CAMBRIDGE

CHECKPOINTS 2018–2022

Year 11 (Stage 6) Physics

- Sample examination questions
- Questions arranged by topic
- Suggested responses to questions

Dr Sydney Boydell
& Dr Eddy de Jong

CAMBRIDGE
UNIVERSITY PRESS

Shaftesbury Road, Cambridge CB2 8EA, United Kingdom

One Liberty Plaza, 20th Floor, New York, NY 10006, USA

477 Williamstown Road, Port Melbourne, VIC 3207, Australia

314–321, 3rd Floor, Plot 3, Splendor Forum, Jasola District Centre, New Delhi – 110025, India

103 Penang Road, #05–06/07, Visioncrest Commercial, Singapore 238467

Cambridge University Press & Assessment is a department of the University of Cambridge.

We share the University's mission to contribute to society through the pursuit of education, learning and research at the highest international levels of excellence.

www.cambridge.org

First published 2018
20 19 18 17 16 15 14 13 12 11 10 9 8 7 6 5

Printed in Australia by Finsbury Green

A catalogue record for this book is available from the National Library of Australia at www.nla.gov.au

ISBN 978-1-108-43529-1 Paperback

Additional resources for this publication at www.cambridge.edu.au/GO

Cambridge University Press & Assessment acknowledges the Aboriginal and Torres Strait Islander peoples of this nation. We acknowledge the traditional custodians of the lands on which our company is located and where we conduct our business. We pay our respects to ancestors and Elders, past and present. Cambridge University Press & Assessment is committed to honouring Aboriginal and Torres Strait Islander peoples' unique cultural and spiritual relationships to the land, waters and seas and their rich contribution to society.

Contents

Preface

This book is a collection of over 550 practice/review questions for the Physics Stage 6 Preliminary course, which commences in 2018.

The questions are intended as pre-examination revision questions, covering the theory concepts of the syllabus with a range of styles and difficulties.

There is more emphasis on questions that require analytical and numerical ability than straight recall, and questions related to practical investigations are largely restricted to graph drawing and analysis of data.

The questions have been grouped in thirteen chapters, with headings aligned to follow the structure of the syllabus.

Answers and outline solutions have been provided to all questions.

Marks have been attached to all questions. This is to indicate the weighting such questions might have in an examination.

Some questions have appeared as questions in IARTV/CSE trial examination papers. The authors are grateful for permission to include these questions in the current book.

Comments and corrections are always welcome from readers; these should be emailed to: sydney@cambridge.org

Syd Boydell

Eddy de Jong

Chapter 1 – Motion in a straight line

Question 1
Compare *distance* and *displacement.*

2 marks

Question 2
Compare *speed* and *velocity*.

2 marks

Question 3
Identify the following quantities as either *vector* or *scalar* quantities.

(a) Time
(b) Distance
(c) Speed
(d) Displacement
(e) Velocity

3 marks

Question 4
Which of the following is closest to the final speed and distance travelled of a ball dropped from a height on Mars that falls for 3.5 s? (Take g_{MARS} = 3.7 m s^{-2})

A. Final speed = 35 m s^{-1}; distance = 61 m
B. Final speed = 35 m s^{-1}; distance = 123 m
C. Final speed = 13 m s^{-1}; distance = 46 m
D. Final speed = 13 m s^{-1}; distance = 23 m

1 mark

Question 5
25 km h^{-1} is closest to which of the following?

A. 6.9 m s^{-1}
B. 69 m s^{-1}
C. 90 m s^{-1}
D. 250 m s^{-1}

1 mark

Question 6
A car accelerates at 2.0 m s^{-2} for 5.0 s. At the end of this time it moves at 30 m s^{-1}.

(a) Which of the following is closest to the distance covered in this time?

A. 20 m
B. 125 m
C. 150 m
D. 175 m

1 mark

(b) Which of the following is closest to the car's speed at t = 5.0 s?

A. 5 m s^{-1}
B. 10 m s^{-1}
C. 15 m s^{-1}
D. 20 m s^{-1}

1 mark

Question 7
A ball is thrown upwards with an initial speed of 25 m s^{-1}. Neglect air resistance.

(a) Which of the following best describes the ball's minimum speed in its flight?

A. Minimum speed = 0 m s^{-1} at t = 2.6 s
B. Minimum speed = 0 m s^{-1} at t = 4.9 s
C. Minimum speed = 10 m s^{-1} at t = 2.6 s
D. Minimum speed = 10 m s^{-1} at t = 4.9 s

1 mark

(b) Which of the following best describes the distance and displacement of the ball during its flight up and down back to its starting point?

A. Distance = 0 m and displacement = 0 m
B. Distance = 32 m and displacement = 32 m
C. Distance = 64 m and displacement = 32 m
D. Distance = 64 m and displacement = 0 m

1 mark

(c) Which of the following best describes the ball's acceleration during its flight?

A. The acceleration direction reverses halfway through the flight.
B. The acceleration direction is constant throughout the flight.
C. The acceleration magnitude decreases during the flight.
D. The acceleration magnitude increases during the flight.

1 mark

Question 8

The speed-time graph below describes the straight-line motion of an object.

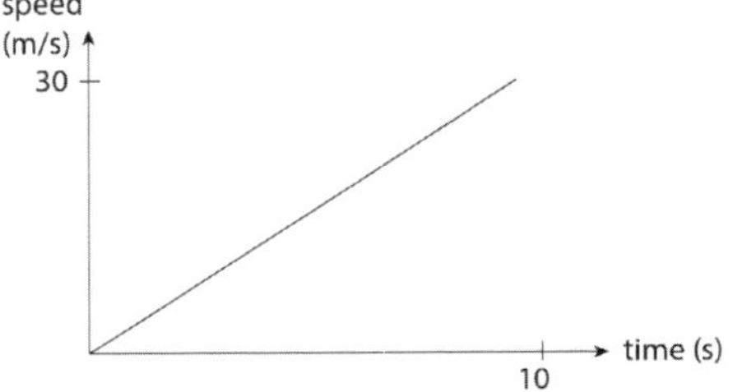

Which of the following best describes the motion of the object at t = 5 s?

A. Speed = 15 m s^{-1} acceleration increasing; distance travelled = 150 m
B. Speed = 15 m s^{-1}; acceleration constant; distance travelled = 38 m
C. Speed = 10 m s^{-1}; acceleration constant; distance travelled = 38 m
D. Speed = 15 m s^{-1}; acceleration constant; distance travelled = 75 m

1 mark

Question 9

The distance-time graph below describes the straight-line motion of an object.

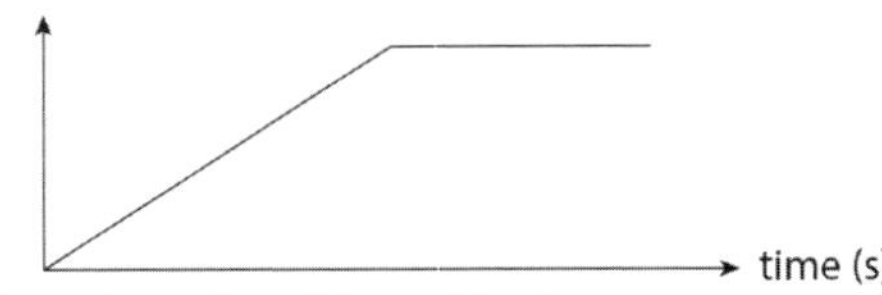

Which of the following best describes this motion?

A. Constant speed followed by no motion.
B. Increasing speed followed by constant speed.
C. Increasing acceleration followed by constant acceleration.
D. Increasing distance followed by constant speed.

1 mark

Question 10

Two trains are each travelling at 40 m s^{-1} towards each other along the same track. When they are 1 km apart, they start to brake, both with a constant deceleration of 1.7 m s^{-2}. Which of the following describes what then happens?

A. The two trains collide.
B. The two trains stop with less than 1 m between them.
C. The two trains stop with about 30 m between them.
D. The two trains stop with about 60 m between them.

1 mark

Question 11

A student competes in a sprint race. Her speed-time graph is shown below.

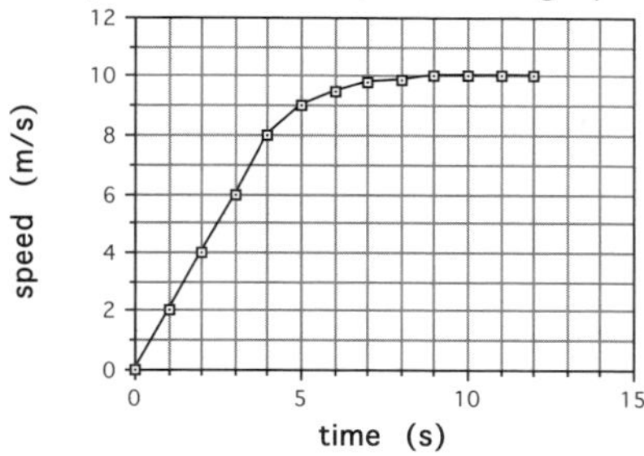

(a) Calculate her average speed over the first three seconds.

1 mark

(b) Calculate the distance she covers in the first 3.0 s.

1 mark

(c) Calculate her change in speed between t = 2.5 s and t = 10.5 s.

1 mark

Question 12

Chris rides his bike along a straight road. For the first 10 s, he accelerates uniformly from 0 m s^{-1} up to 12 m s^{-1}. He then rides at constant speed for 20 s, before slowing to 6 m s^{-1} uniformly in a time of 4 s. He then rides at constant speed for the next 6 s. Draw a speed-time line graph of Chris's motion. Label the axes correctly.

4 marks

Question 13

A car accelerates in a straight line. Its speed-time is shown below.

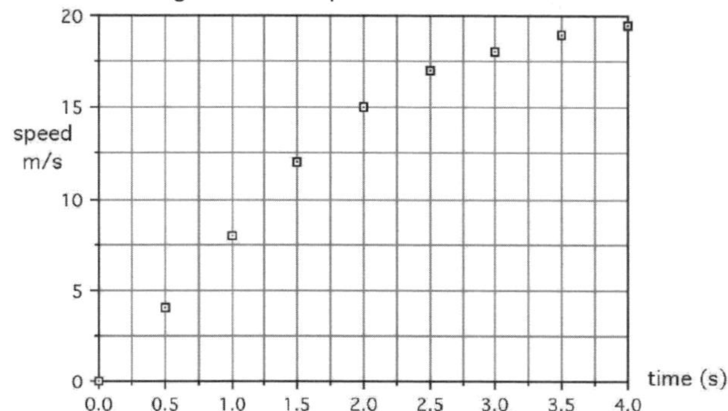

(a) Estimate when the car first breaks the suburban speed limit of 50 km h^{-1}.

2 marks

(b) Estimate the distance travelled by the car in the first 4.0 seconds.

2 marks

Question 14

A cross-country runner runs in a straight line. The table below shows how her speed (v) changes with time (t) over a 360 s time interval.

t (s)	0	30	60	90	120	150	180	210	240	270	300	330	360
v (m s^{-1})	4	4	4	3	3	3	3.5	4	5.5	7	5	3	1

(a) Graph her speed against time. Make sure that your graph has clearly labelled axes. Include a trend line of best fit.

4 marks

(b) From your graph, calculate the distance she covers between t = 0 and t = 60 s.

1 mark

Question 15

A skydiver steps out of a hot air balloon high above the ground and falls vertically. His speed varies with time as shown below. He doesn't open his parachute straight away.

Time (s)	Speed (m s^{-1})	Time (s)	Speed (m s^{-1})
0	0	10	65
1	10	11	65
2	20	12	65
3	29	13	30
4	37	14	5
5	44	15	5
6	50	16	5
7	55	17	5
8	59	18	5
9	62	19 & 20	5

(a) Graph these values. Label the axes correctly. Draw a line of best fit.

4 marks

(b) Calculate the terminal speed of the parachutist *before* he opens the parachute.

1 mark

(c) Calculate the terminal speed of the parachutist *after* he opens the parachute.

1 mark

(d) Using the graph, estimate the distance he falls from $t = 0$ to $t = 20$ s.

3 marks

(e) Which of the following is closest to the time that he opens his parachute?

A. 10 s
B. 13 s
C. 15 s
D. 20 s

1 mark

(f) Use your answers to estimate his average speed during his 20 s descent.

1 mark

Question 16

A 400 m runner is competing in a time trial on a circular track. The circumference of the track is exactly 400 m, and she starts exactly where she finishes. She takes 48 seconds to complete her run. Calculate her average speed during the time trial.

2 marks

Question 17

A snail crawls along a straight line path. The displacement-time graph is shown on the next page.

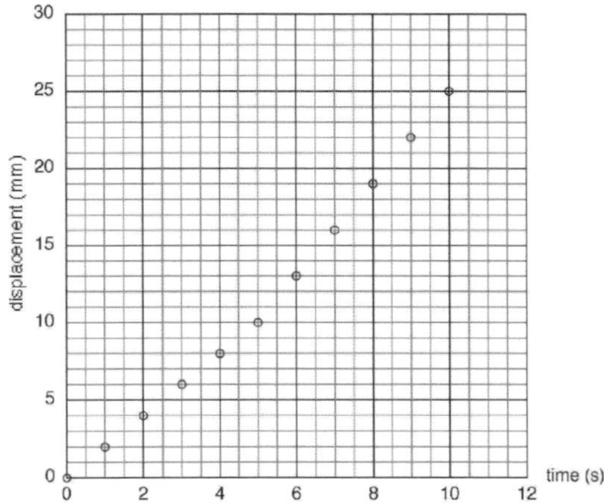

(a) Calculate the speed of the snail at time $t = 2.5$ s.

2 marks

(b) Calculate the speed of the snail at time $t = 9.0$ s.

2 marks

(c) Calculate the average speed of the snail over the first 10 s of its motion.

2 marks

Question 18

A ball is thrown straight upwards in the air on a remote planet, where the acceleration due to gravity is *not* the same as the value on Earth. There is no significant air resistance. The graph of its *displacement* against time is shown below.

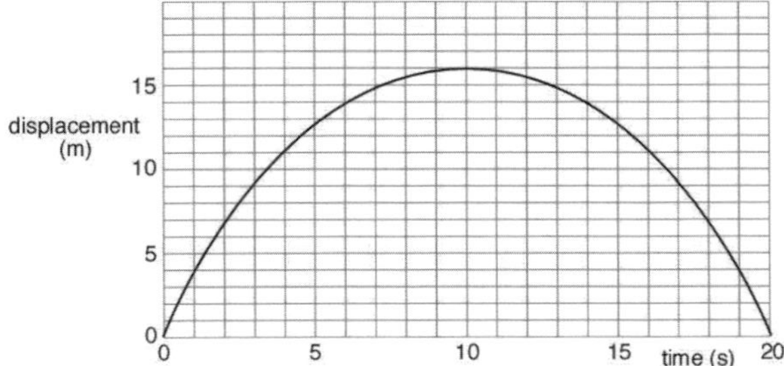

(a) Use the graph to compare its velocity at the start of its 'flight' with its velocity at the end of the 'flight'.

2 marks

(b) Calculate the average velocity of the ball during the first 10 s of its motion.

2 marks

(c) State what the graph tells you about the velocity of the ball at time $t = 10$ s.

2 marks

(d) Sketch a graph of the *distance* against time for the ball's 'flight'.

3 marks

Question 19

An older marathon runner completes the 42.2 km distance in a time of 4 h 45 min. Express his average speed in units of both m s^{-1} and also km h^{-1}.

2 marks

Question 20

A swimmer in an event starts at 2.0 m s^{-1} for 1.0 km., then at 1.0 m s^{-1} for the next km., and the last 500 m at 0.5 m s^{-1}. She changes speed suddenly.

(a) Calculate the time she takes to swim the entire event.

3 marks

(b) Calculate the average speed she swims the entire event.

2 marks

(c) Sketch the distance-time graph for the swimmer during the event. Label the axes correctly. Draw a trendline of best fit.

3 marks

(d) Sketch the speed-time graph for the swimmer during the event. Label the axes correctly. Draw a line of best fit.

3 marks

Question 21

Visitors in a hotel room see a cat falling past their window. The speed of the cat at the top of the window is 3.0 m s^{-1}; by the time the cat passes the bottom of the window it is travelling at 5.0 m s^{-1}. Neglect air resistance.

(a) Calculate the height of the window.

2 marks

(b) 0.50 s after passing the bottom of the window, the cat lands safely on the ground. Calculate the height of the bottom of the window from the ground.

2 marks

Question 22

During a physical education class, Alice steps off the 3 m diving board.

(a) Students measure the acceleration due to gravity by timing Alice's fall. When she steps, she takes 0.80 s to reach the water (measured with a stopwatch). Calculate g from this. Give your answer to one significant figure.

2 marks

(b) At what speed is Alice travelling *just before* she reaches the water? Use the value for g calculated in part (a).

2 marks

(c) Another student (Hazel) climbs to the board, but this time, she leaps vertically upwards at a speed of 4.0 m s^{-1}. At what speed will she reach the water below? Use the value for g calculated in part (a).

3 marks

Question 23

State the relative velocities of the following objects, giving magnitude and direction. Give the relative velocity of the first object relative to the second object.

(a) A car moving right at 20 m s^{-1} overtakes a car moving right at 17 m s^{-1}.

1 mark

(b) A car moving right at 16 m s^{-1} is passed by a car moving right at 21 m s^{-1}.

1 mark

(c) A runner moving N at 4 m s^{-1} approaches another runner moving S at 4 m s^{-1}.

1 mark

(d) A stationary balloon is approached by an aeroplane moving E at 80 m s^{-1}.

1 mark

Question 24

Students are asked to measure the local acceleration of gravity by throwing a basketball vertically into the air in a classroom. A motion sensor measures the speed that the ball starts moving upwards (v_1) and the speed that it returns to its starting height (v_2), and a timing device measures the time interval between these two events (t). The timing device has a measurement uncertainty of $\pm$ 0.05 s.

(a) Compare the expected values that could be obtained for v_1 and v_2.

2 marks

(b) Outline how these measurements can be used to calculate the free fall acceleration of gravity.

2 marks

(c) Without changing the apparatus, discuss how the accuracy of the result could be improved.

3 marks

Question 25

Students use a high-speed camera to measure the position of a model car as it accelerates along a 10 m long straight track. This allows them to measure the position of the car every 0.1 s. Discuss how they could measure

(a) the average speed of the car as it completes its journey along the 10 m track.

2 marks

(b) the instantaneous speed at a specific time during the journey.

2 marks

Question 26

Students are given the following method for measuring the free fall acceleration of gravity. They use a golf ball, a metre ruler and a manually operated timer. Their reaction time is known to be ± 0.1 s.

1 Measure a height of 1.0 m using a metre ruler.
2 Drop a golf ball from 1.0 m; measure the time for the drop using a stopwatch.
3 Record the time taken for the fall.
4 Repeat the measurements for heights of 2.0 m, 3.0 m, 4.0 m, and 5.0 m.
5 State all data in SI units.
6 Calculate the free fall acceleration of the golf ball using a constant acceleration formula.

(a) Identify the best constant acceleration formula to use.

2 marks

(b) Critically analyse the uncertainty involved in the recommended measurements.

4 marks

(c) Suggest *two* improvements to the experimental method (using the same apparatus) that would be likely to improve the accuracy of the result.

2 marks

Chapter 2 – Motion on a plane

Question 1

A model train travels around a circular track of radius 1.0 m at a speed of 2.0 m s^{-1}.

(a) Which *one or more* of the following best describes the displacement of the train in one revolution of the track?

A. The displacement is zero.
B. The displacement has a magnitude of 2π metres.
C. The displacement has a magnitude of 4π metres.
D. The displacement has a magnitude of $2.0 \times$ the time taken.

1 mark

(b) Which *one or more* of the following best describes the displacement of the train when it has completed one half revolution of the track?

A. The displacement is zero.
B. The displacement has a magnitude of 2π metres.
C. The displacement has a magnitude of 2.0 metres.
D. The displacement has a magnitude of 4.0 metres.

1 mark

(c) Which *one or more* of the following best describes the velocity of the train during one complete revolution of the track?

A. The velocity is unchanged.
B. The magnitude of the velocity is constant.
C. The direction of the velocity changes.
D. The velocity of the train at the end is the same as at the start.

1 mark

Question 2

A player swings hard at a baseball and sends it a long way. The diagram is from the perspective of a passing bird high overhead.

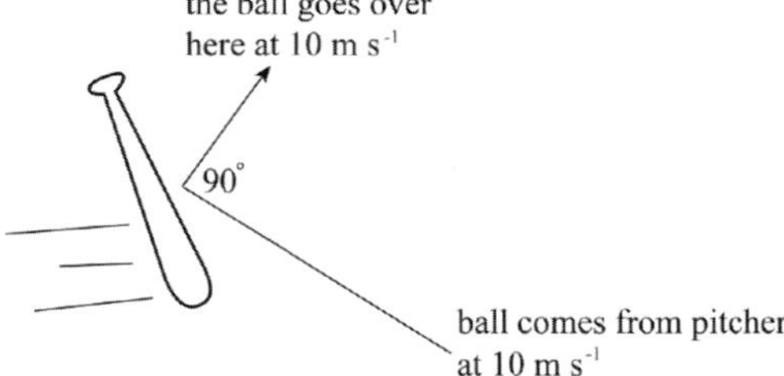

Which of the arrows in the diagram below best describes the direction of the *change* in the velocity of the ball?

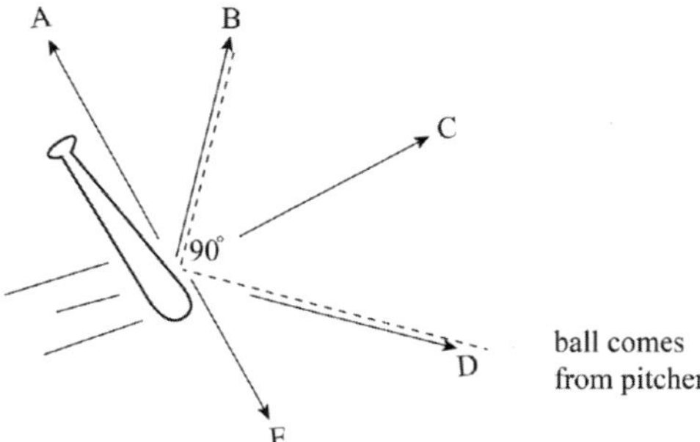

1 mark

Question 3

A toy car runs off the end of a horizontal table and falls to the floor below. Air resistance can be neglected.

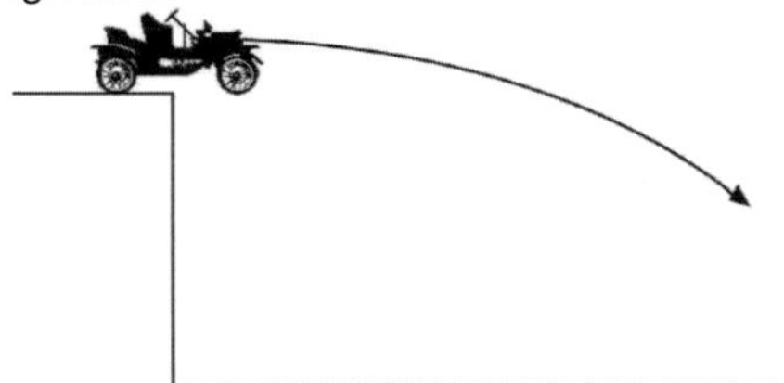

Which *one or more* of the following best describes the vertical and horizontal components of the velocity (v_V and v_H) during the 'flight' of the car?

A. At the start, v_V is zero.
B. At the start, v_H is zero.
C. During the flight, v_V increases.
D. During the flight, the vector sum of V_V and v_H is constant.

1 mark

Question 4

Two boats in an ocean race pass within sight of each other. One (the *Mary*) is heading SW at 10 m s^{-1}; the other (the *Celeste*) is heading NW, also at 10 m s^{-1}.

(a) Which of the following best describes the direction of the *Mary* relative to the *Celeste?*

A. South
B. North
C. South-west
D. West

1 mark

(b) Which of the following best describes the direction of the *Celeste* relative to the *Mary?*

A. South
B. North
C. South-west
D. East

1 mark

(c) Which of the following is closest to the magnitude of the relative velocity of the boats relative to each other?

A. 7 m s^{-1}
B. 10 m s^{-1}
C. 14 m s^{-1}
D. 20 m s^{-1}

1 mark

Question 5

Two cars (A and B) are approaching an intersection as shown in the diagram below. They are travelling at the same speed.

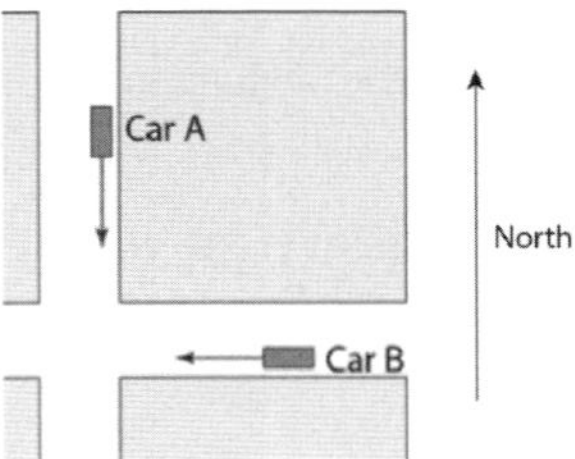

(a) Which of the following best describes the direction of the velocity of Car A relative to Car B?

A. South
B. South-west
C. South-east
D. East

1 mark

(b) Which of the following best describes the direction of the velocity of Car B relative to Car A?

A. North
B. North-west
C. North-east
D. West

1 mark

(c) If the two cars are both travelling at 54 km h^{-1}, which of the following is closest to the magnitude of their relative velocity to each other?

A. 15 m s^{-1}
B. 21 m s^{-1}
C. 36 m s^{-1}
D. 54 m s^{-1}

1 mark

Question 6

A rocket is travelling in deep space in a straight line with its main motors switched off. An alien spacecraft switches on a 'tractor beam' (at point Q) that causes a significant acceleration at right angles to the rocket's original direction. Which of the diagrams below best shows the likely path of the rocket?

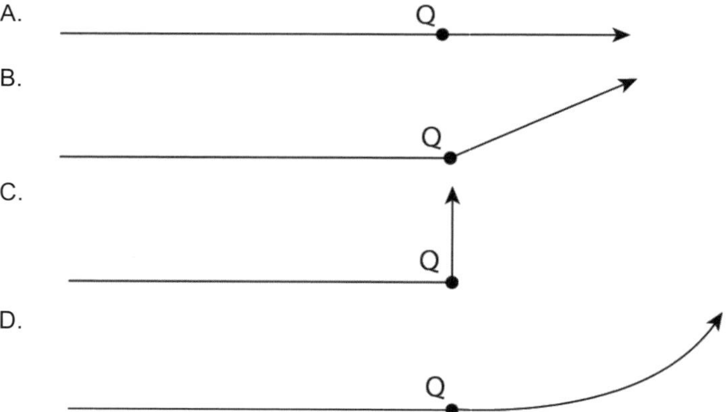

1 mark

Question 7

An ant moves 90 cm North in 2 minutes and then 120 cm East in the next 2 minutes.

(a) Calculate the average speed of the ant over this time, in units of m min^{-1}.

2 marks

(b) Calculate the magnitude of the displacement of the ant over this time. Give your answer in cm.

2 marks

(c) Calculate the magnitude of the average velocity of the ant over this time. Give your answer in cm s^{-1}.

2 marks

Question 8

The two vectors in the diagram represent physical quantities. Vector ***a*** is in the *x*-direction, with magnitude of 10 units. Vector ***b*** has magnitude of 20 units.

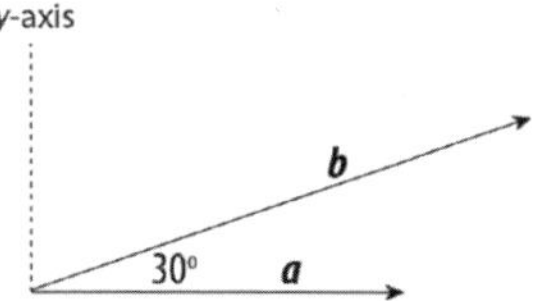

(a) Calculate the size of the *x*-component of ***b***.

2 marks

(b) Calculate the size of the *y*-component of ***b***.

2 marks

(c) Calculate the size of the *y*-component of vector ***a***.

1 mark

(d) Calculate the magnitude of vector (***a*** + ***b***).

2 marks

(e) Calculate the direction of vector (***a*** + ***b***), anti-clockwise from the *x*-axis.

3 marks

Question 9

The diagram below shows two velocity vectors ***a*** and ***b***. They are perpendicular to each other. Vectors have magnitude: ***a*** = 24 m s^{-1} and vector ***b*** = 32 m s^{-1}.

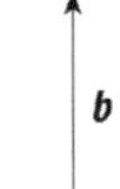

a

(a) Calculate the magnitude of (***a*** + ***b***).

2 marks

(b) Calculate the direction of (***a*** + ***b***), as an anti-clockwise angle from ***a***.

2 marks

(c) Calculate the magnitude of (***b*** – ***a***).

2 marks

(d) Calculate the direction of (***b*** – ***a***), as an anti-clockwise angle from ***a***.

2 marks

(e) Calculate the magnitude of (***a*** + 2***b***).

2 marks

(f) Calculate the direction of (***a*** + 2***b***), as an anti-clockwise angle from ***a***.

2 marks

Question 10

Sam rides his bike at constant speed on a flat road, as shown. At P he drops his coffee container. It lands in a bin at Q, 3.0 m below the road that he rides along.

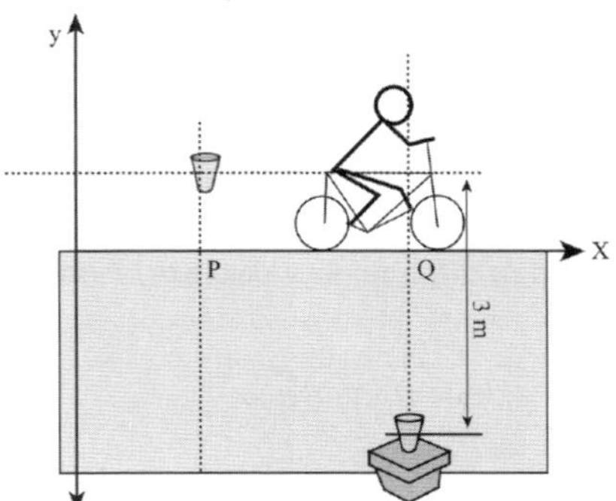

(a) Describe the path of the coffee container relative to Sam and also to an observer standing beside the recycling bin.

4 marks

(b) Calculate the time it takes for Sam to ride from point P to point Q.

2 marks

Question 11

A netball player shoots for goal. The path of the ball is sketched below.

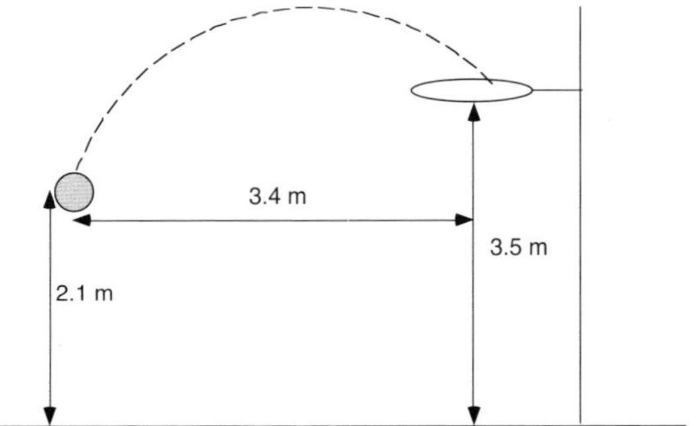

(a) What is the vertical displacement involved in the flight of the ball?

2 marks

(b) What is the total displacement involved in the flight?

2 marks

(c) The ball takes 1.1 s for its flight. What is the horizontal component of its velocity?

2 marks

(d) What is the vertical component of its launch velocity?

3 marks

(e) What is its launch speed?

2 marks

(f) At what angle to the horizontal was it launched?

2 marks

Question 12

A motorboat is crossing a river, as shown in the diagram. It is pointing in a direction perpendicular to the riverbank, as shown. However, it moves in the direction shown by the dashed line in the diagram.

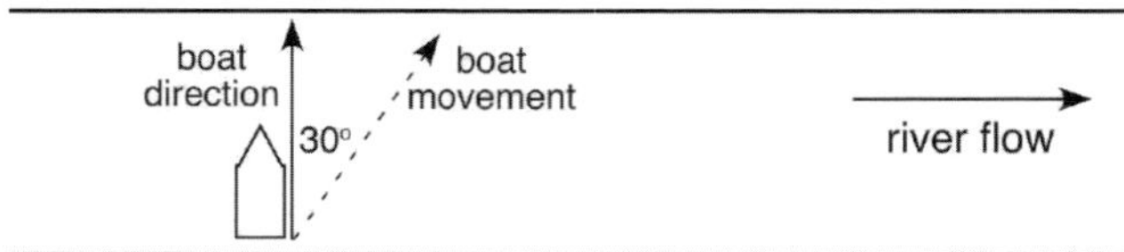

(a) Explain, using vector concepts, why the boat does *not* travel perpendicular to the bank.

3 marks

The angle between where the boat points and the direction the boat moves is 30°. The time to cross a 100 m wide river is 11.5 s. The engine operates at full power.

(b) Show that the speed of the boat in a still lake, if operating at the same power, would be 8.7 m s^{-1}.

2 marks

(c) Calculate the speed of flow of the river.

3 marks

Question 13

An aeroplane is approaching an airport. It is travelling at a *speed* of 200 m s^{-1}. It is gradually losing altitude. The horizontal component of its velocity is 199 m s^{-1}.

(a) Calculate the angle between the horizontal and the velocity of the aeroplane.

2 marks

(b) Calculate the (downward) vertical component of its velocity.

2 marks

Question 14

A light aeroplane is flying North at its maximum airspeed of 70 m s^{-1} on a day when there is no crosswind.

(a) When it encounters a 20 m s^{-1} crosswind from the West (towards East), the pilot notices that the aeroplane's speed relative to the ground increases. Calculate the size of this increase (answer to two significant figures).

2 marks

(b) The pilot also notices that the direction of the aeroplane's path over the ground changes. Calculate the angle between the original northerly direction and the new direction (answer in degrees to two significant figures).

2 marks

(c) The pilot adjusts the direction that the aeroplane heads so that the path over the ground returns to northerly. By how much does she adjust the direction of aeroplane? (Answer in degrees to two significant figures.)

3 marks

Chapter 3 – Forces, acceleration

Question 1

A large jet airliner is in level flight at constant speed in a straight line. The weight of the airliner is exactly balanced by the upward lift force on the wings. Which of the following best describes the relationship between the thrust (forward force) of the engines and the drag (backwards force of air resistance)?

A. The thrust is slightly greater than the drag.
B. The thrust is considerably greater than the drag.
C. The thrust is sometimes larger and sometimes smaller than the drag.
D. The thrust and drag are exactly equal.

1 mark

Question 2

A skier is sliding down a gentle slope of soft snow. She is travelling down the slope at constant speed. Which of the following best describes why her speed is not changing?

A. The friction from the snow balances the downhill component of her weight.
B. The gravity component down the hill is not strong enough to accelerate her.
C. The friction of the snow is equal to her weight.
D. The slope is not steep enough for any acceleration to occur.

1 mark

Question 3

An aeroplane in flight has a mass of 40 000 kg and a constant velocity of 300 m s^{-1}.

(a) Which of the following is closest to the magnitude of the *lift force* on the wings?

A. 0 N
B. 30 000 N
C. 40 000 N
D. 400 000 N

1 mark

(b) Which of the following is closest to the magnitude of the net force acting on the aeroplane?

A. 0 N
B. 30 000 N
C. 40 000 N
D. 400 000 N

1 mark

Question 4

The acceleration due to gravity on the Moon is about 1.6 m s^{-2}. This means that (*one or more answers*)

A. the free fall acceleration of objects on the Moon's surface depends on their weight.
B. the free fall acceleration of objects on the Moon's surface depends on their mass.
C. both mass and weight of objects on the Moon's surface are less than their mass and weight on Earth's surface.
D. the weight of objects on the Moon's surface is less than on Earth's surface, but their mass remains unchanged.

1 mark

Question 5

(a) Jim has a mass of 60 kg. He is running slowly along a track in a straight line at constant speed. Which *one or more* of the following best describes the frictional forces between his shoes and the ground?

A. Friction between Jim's shoes and the ground is in the direction he is running.
B. Frictional forces always act in the opposite direction of any motion.
C. There is a considerable amount of air resistance acting vertically on Jim.
D. Jim can run faster on slippery ground than on rough ground because the friction forces from slippery ground are smaller.

1 mark

Jim now increases his speed by pushing harder backwards on the ground. He exerts a frictional force of 50 N on the ground. As a result, he accelerates at 0.5 m s^{-2}.

(b) Which of the following values is closest to the forward friction force acting on Jim's shoes?

A. 0 N
B. 30 N
C. 50 N
D. 588 N

1 mark

(c) Which of the following is closest to the net force acting on Jim as he accelerates?

A. 0 N
B. 30 N
C. 50 N
D. 588 N

1 mark

Question 6

A student leans against a wall after a gruelling Physics class. The friction on her feet stops her feet sliding. The diagram on the right models the situation on the left.

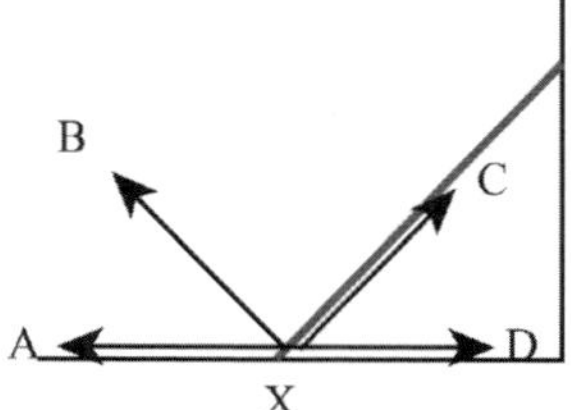

(a) Which of the forces (represented by arrows) in the right-hand diagram best shows the direction of the friction force acting on her feet?

1 mark

(b) Which of the following best represents the sum of all the forces acting on the student *with the exception* of her weight force?

A. A force directed vertically upwards.
B. A force directed vertically downwards.
C. A force directed to her left.
D. A force directed to her right.

1 mark

Question 7

Thomasina the engine moves slowly along a flat track at constant speed. The total of all the forces *opposing* her motion is 275 N. Which of the following best describes the total of frictional forces acting on Thomasina's wheels? (Ignore rolling friction.)

A. Friction between her wheels and the track is in the same direction she is moving.
B. Frictional forces always act in the opposite direction of any motion.
C. There is a considerable amount of air resistance acting on her.
D. She could travel faster on slippery rails than on rough rails because the friction forces are smaller.

1 mark

Question 8

The arrows in the following diagram show possible *forces* acting on a cricket ball, after being hit by a bat. The ball is moving horizontally to the *right.*

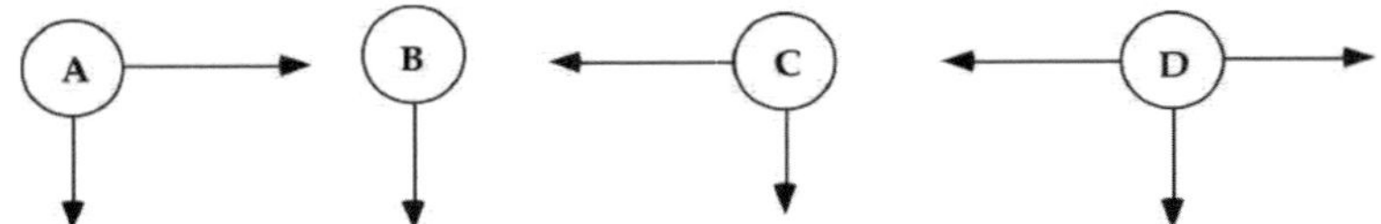

(a) Which diagram above best describes a cricket ball moving with very little air resistance?

1 mark

(b) Which diagram above best describes a cricket ball moving with substantial air resistance?

1 mark

Question 9

A tennis ball bounce is shown below. Before the ball hits the ground, it is not spinning. After contact with the ground, it is spinning, as shown.

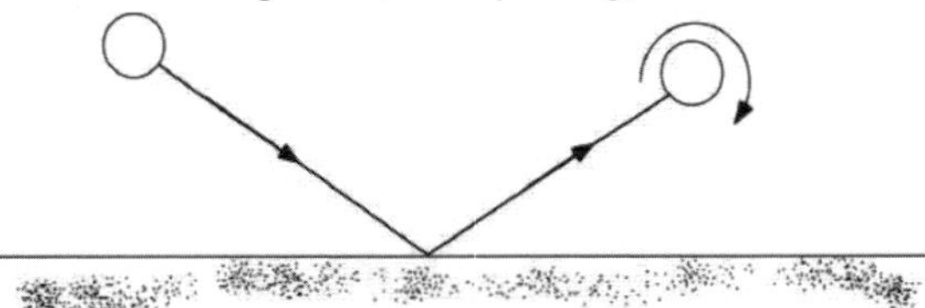

Which of the options below best gives the reason why the ball is spinning?

A. Friction exerted a force on the ball towards the right.
B. The normal reaction exerted a force on the ball towards the right.
C. Friction exerted a force on the ball towards the left.
D. The normal reaction exerted a force on the ball towards the left.

1 mark

Question 10

When a low density polystyrene ball is dropped from a height of over 10 m, its speed is likely to approach a *terminal* value (maximum falling speed). At terminal speed, identify the forces acting on the ball. Give their direction(s) and relative magnitude(s).

3 marks

Question 11

In order to accelerate or decelerate, a runner must be acted on by *external* forces that cause such changes in motion. Identify the main force that causes the runner below to *accelerate*. On the sketch below show the *point of action* of the force, with an arrow to indicate its direction.

2 marks

Question 12

A bicyclist decelerates her bike by applying the brakes *on the front wheel only*. The forces acting on the bicycle and its rider *while it is decelerating* include weight (*mg*), normal reaction forces on each wheel (N_{FRONT} and N_{BACK}), air resistance (*AR*) and static friction (*SF*). Label the sketch below with each of these listed forces. (Ignore rolling friction.)

3 marks

Questions 13

Phan is running up a hill at constant speed. He has a mass of 66 kg.

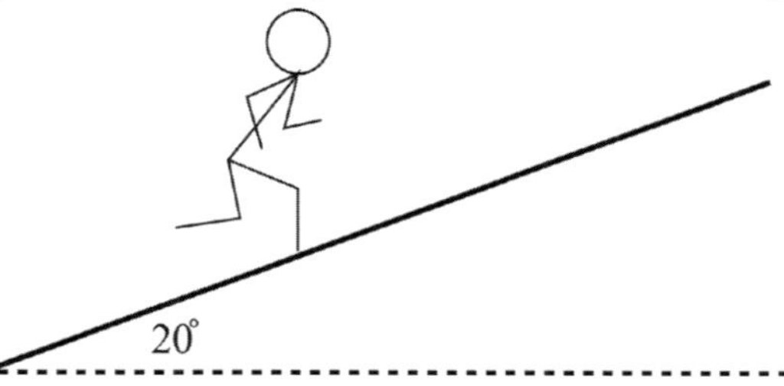

(a) Calculate Phan's *weight*. Give your answer in newton.

2 marks

(b) Calculate the component of his weight down the slope.

2 marks

(c) Explain why the net force on Phan is zero, in terms of the various forces acting on him.

3 marks

(d) Calculate the normal reaction force between Phan and the slope.

3 marks

(e) Phan is making use of static friction to help him run up the hill. Assuming that air resistance is negligible, calculate the size of the static friction force up the slope.

2 marks

Question 14

A bike rider is going as fast as he can along a flat road. He is pushing as hard as he can on the pedals. Explain why he is not accelerating, in terms of the various forces acting on him and his bike.

3 marks

Question 15

Descending a section of a ski slope, a skier moves down a 35° slope. She stops halfway down; her situation is modelled by the diagram below. Her weight is 637 N.

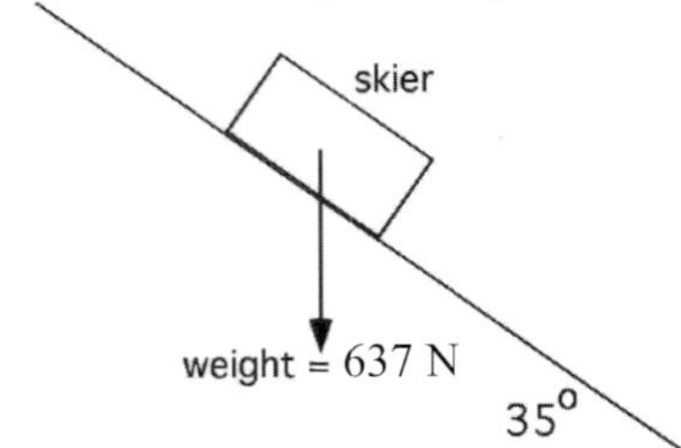

(a) Calculate the skier's mass.

1 mark

(b) State the sum of all the forces acting on her while standing still on the slope.

1 mark

(c) If the slope is at 35 degrees to the horizontal, as shown, find the value of the friction force acting on her while she is stationary.

2 marks

(d) She then faces down the slope, and allows herself to slide straight down the slope. Neglect friction and air resistance forces. Calculate her acceleration.

2 marks

Question 16

A rock climber is stationary on a rock-face. He has a mass of 60 kg. His situation is modelled by the force diagram on the right below.

(a) Identify the three forces in the diagram. Write their names on the arrows on the diagram. Use forces from this list: *gravity, friction, air resistance, normal reaction force, inertia, tension.*

3 marks

(b) Calculate the net force acting on the climber.

2 marks

(c) The rock-face makes an angle of 70 degrees with the horizontal, as shown. Calculate the magnitude of the force acting straight up the rock-face.

2 marks

(d) If the force acting straight up the rock-face were removed, the climber would start to move down the rock-face. Explain why, in terms of the forces still acting on him.

2 marks

(e) Ignoring friction, calculate his acceleration in the case of no friction.

2 marks

Question 17

During a drive in the country, a driver encounters the situations below. For each of them, identify:

(a) whether there is a non-zero net force acting on the car
(b) whether the car is accelerating
(c) the horizontal forces acting on the car

Situation 1
The car accelerates from rest in a straight line.

Situation 2
The car is travelling at constant speed along a flat road.

Situation 3
The car is travelling down a hill, slowly gaining speed, but the driver's foot is not on the accelerator or the brake.

Situation 4
The car is travelling around a corner at constant speed on a flat road.

Situation 5
The driver applies the brakes on an icy stretch of flat road and the car skids to a stop.

Situation 6
The car is parked on a hill with the handbrake firmly applied.

6 marks

Question 18

Between the Earth and the Moon there is a point in space where the gravitational field of the Earth exactly balances the gravitational field of the Moon. A shuttle navigates to this point. Compare the *mass* and *weight* of the satellite at this point.

2 marks

Question 19

Fred skis from rest at the top of a slope and slides a distance of 60 m. The slope makes an angle of 18° with the horizontal. The slope is very icy and the effects of friction (including air resistance) may be ignored. He has a mass of 80 kg.

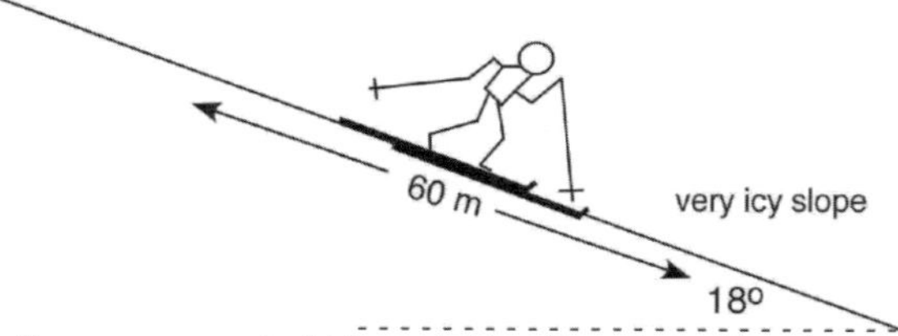

(a) Calculate the component of his weight acting down the slope.

2 marks

(b) Calculate the normal reaction force that the icy surface exerts on Fred.

2 marks

(c) Calculate the net force on Fred.

2 marks

(d) Calculate the acceleration of Fred as he slides freely down the icy slope.

2 marks

Question 20

A trainee diver is held in a supporting mechanism to enable 'dry-land' training. The arrangement can be modelled by the arrangement shown in the sketch below. The supporting ropes make an angle of 50° to the horizontal.

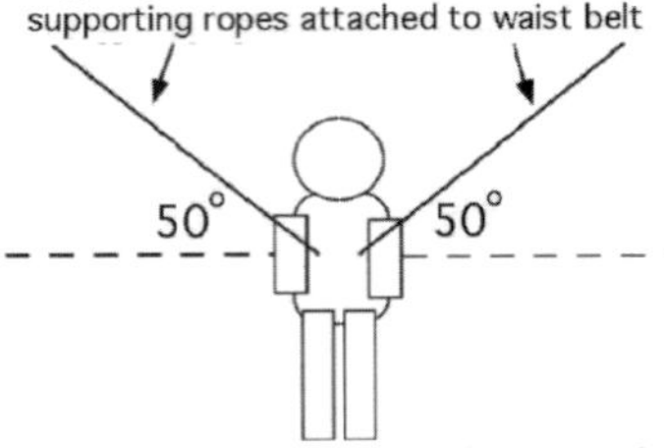

If the mass of the trainee diver is 65 kg, calculate the tension in each of the supporting ropes.

3 marks

Question 21

A car is being towed out of a bog by two ropes as shown below. The tension in each rope is equal to 2000 N.

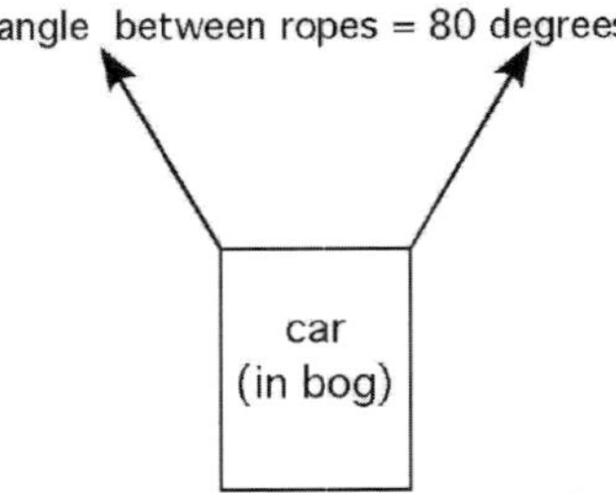

The car is moving slowly at a constant speed of 2 m s^{-1} out of the bog. Calculate the total frictional force acting on the car as it moves out of the bog.

3 marks

Question 22

When a person jumps up from the ground (for example a high jumper), the normal reaction force between the person's feet and the ground is for a short time significantly greater than the person's weight. Use Newton's laws to explain why.

4 marks

Question 23

A cyclist is riding up a hill, slowly, on her bike. She is travelling at constant speed.

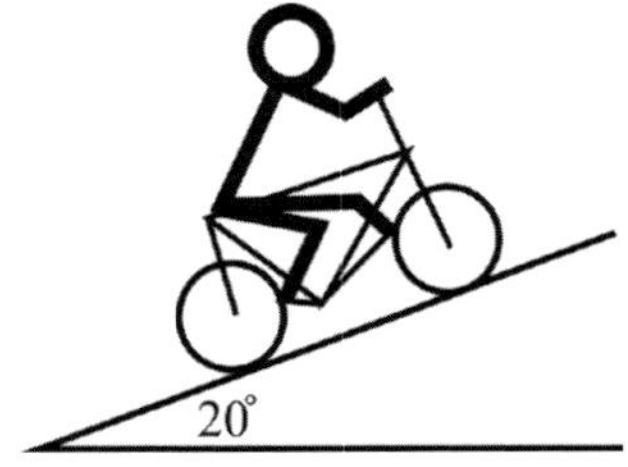

(a) Draw labelled arrows representing the forces acting on the combination of the cyclist and her bike. You can neglect air resistance (she is cycling very slowly).

2 marks

(b) The cyclist and her bike have a total mass of 75 kg, and the hill makes an angle of 20° to the horizontal. Calculate the size of the net force acting on the combination of the cyclist and bike.

2 marks

Question 24

A car accelerates steadily along a straight road. The forward force between the tyres and road is 1120 N; the car has a mass of 500 kg. It accelerates at 0.60 m s^{-2}.

(a) Calculate the total of the retarding forces acting on the car (these come from air resistance, rolling friction, and friction in various bearings).

3 marks

(b) The driver applies the brakes, and the car slows down at a rate of 3.0 m s^{-2}. The retarding friction forces of part (a) are still present, but now there is an additional retarding force between the road and the tyres. Calculate the size of this retarding force.

3 marks

Question 25

A car towing a trailer along a road is accelerating at 1.0 m s^{-2}. Take opposing friction as zero. The tension in the coupling between the car and the trailer is 1000 N.

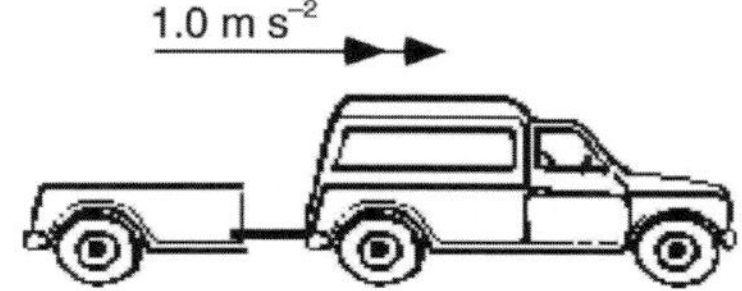

(a) Calculate the mass of the trailer.

2 marks

(b) If the mass of the car is 1500 kg, calculate the driving force that the wheels exert on the road.

2 marks

(c) Calculate the forward frictional force that the road is exerting on the car's driving wheels.

2 marks

Chapter 4 – Forces, energy

Question 1

The collision between two 2.0 kg balls can be modelled by two isolated masses colliding.

(a) Which of the following best describes the kinetic energy before and after the collision?

A. The kinetic energy increases by 1.5 J.
B. The kinetic energy decreases by 1.5 J.
C. The kinetic energy remains constant at 4.0 J.
D. The kinetic energy remains constant at 2.5 J.

1 mark

(b) This collision could best be described as

A. an elastic collision.
B. an inelastic collision.
C. a partially elastic collision.
D. a completely inelastic collision.

1 mark

Question 2

Cycling uphill involves the conversion of energy from one form to another.

(a) Which of the following statements is the most accurate expression of this?

A. Chemical energy is converted directly to kinetic energy.
B. Chemical energy is converted directly to thermal energy.
C. Chemical energy is converted directly to gravitational potential energy.
D. Chemical energy is converted to thermal energy and kinetic energy.

1 mark

(b) In a race, Flossie calculates that she 'burns' a total of 450 kJ of chemical energy. The race lasts 10 minutes. Which of the following is closest to her average power consumption of Flossie during the race?

A. 0.75 W
B. 45 W
C. 750 W
D. 4500 W

1 mark

Question 3

Jimmie is trying to reduce his weight by eating less and exercising more. He uses an exercise bike. While he is pedalling on it, he generates 1.20 kW. Of this, 25.0% ends up as mechanical work; the rest is dissipated as thermal energy in his body.

Which of the following is closest to the number of kilojoules of thermal energy that he produces in his body if he exercises on his bike for 8.00 minutes?

A. 0.432 kJ
B. 7.20 kJ
C. 144 kJ
D. 432 kJ

1 mark

Question 4

A pole-vaulter achieves much of her height by converting stored elastic energy in the pole into gravitational potential energy. Her mass is 60 kg. She wants to vault a bar 7.1 m high. 90% of her potential energy needs to come from the elastic potential energy in the pole. Which of the following is closest to the amount of elastic potential energy that needs to be stored in the pole? (Treat the person as a point mass.)

A. 0.43 kJ
B. 0.47 kJ
C. 4.2 kJ
D. 4.6 kJ

1 mark

Question 5

A car of weight 5000 N drives up a hill of gradient 30° at a constant speed of 15 m s^{-1}. The driving force exerted by the wheels is equal to 2700 N. The tyres do not slip.

(a) Which of the following is closest to the power output of the car engine?

A. 20 kW
B. 38 kW
C. 41 kW
D. 50 kW

1 mark

(b) Which of the following is closest to the *retarding* friction forces action on the car?

A. 200.0 N
B. 2500 N
C. 2700 N
D. 5000 N

1 mark

(c) If the efficiency of the car engine is 20%, which of the following is closest to the chemical energy required for the car to develop mechanical power of 50 kW for one hour?

A. 3.00 MJ
B. 15.0 MJ
C. 180 MJ
D. 900 MJ

1 mark

Question 6

A block of wood is dragged up an inclined plane at a steady speed of 1.5 m s^{-1}.

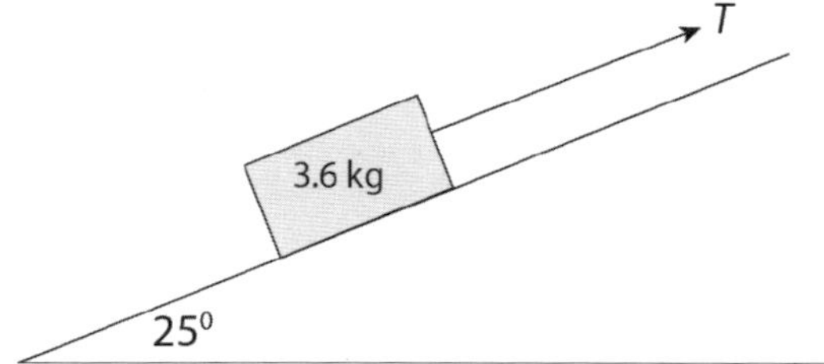

(a) If friction is ignored, which of the following is closest to the tension, T, in the cable dragging the block?

A. 0.4 N
B. 1.0 N
C. 10 N
D. 21 N

1 mark

(b) If friction is present, with μ = 0.65, which of the following is closest to the retarding force due to this friction?

A. 1.0 N
B. 2.1 N
C. 9.7 N
D. 21 N

1 mark

Question 7

Jacinta works out in the gym, lifting 7 kg weights through a vertical distance of 70 cm in a 'shoulder press' exercise. She completes 12 repetitions of the exercise in 30 s.

(a) Which of the following is closest to the total amount of mechanical work she does in this time?

A. 50.0 J
B. 60.0 J
C. 400 J
D. 580 J

1 mark

(b) Which of the following is closest to the average mechanical power she generates in this time?

A. 1.5 W
B. 2.0 W
C. 15 W
D. 20 W

1 mark

Question 8

A 10 kg block of wood on an inclined plane, as shown, does not slip down the slope.

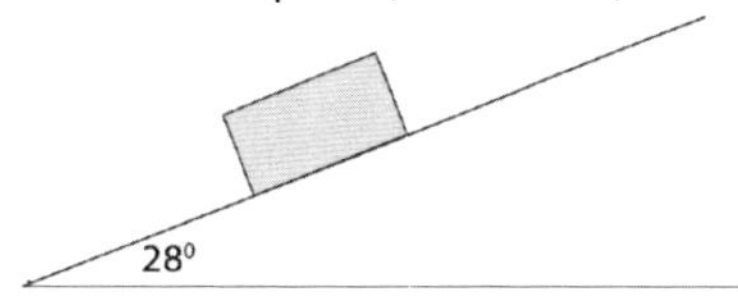

(a) Which of the following is closest to the normal reaction force on the 10 kg block?

A. 8.8 N
B. 46 N
C. 87 N
D. 98 N

1 mark

(b) Which of the following is closest to the net force acting on the 10 kg block?

A. 0 N
B. 46 N
C. 87 N
D. 98 N

1 mark

(c) Students find that if the angle is larger than 28° then the block slides. Which of the following is closest to the coefficient of friction μ between the block and the plane?

A. 0.33
B. 0.47
C. 0.53
D. 0.88

1 mark

Question 9

A basketball player bounces a 450 g ball on the court floor. Just before the ball hits the ground, it is travelling at 8 m s^{-1}. After it bounces, it leaves the floor at 6 m s^{-1}.

(a) Calculate how much kinetic energy has been converted into other forms of energy during this bounce.

2 marks

(b) 'Energy cannot be created or destroyed.' Account for the 'missing' kinetic energy in terms of this statement.

3 marks

Question 10

A train of mass 600 kg travels up a hill at a constant speed of 10 m s^{-1}. The only friction is between the track and the driving wheels. There is no retarding friction.

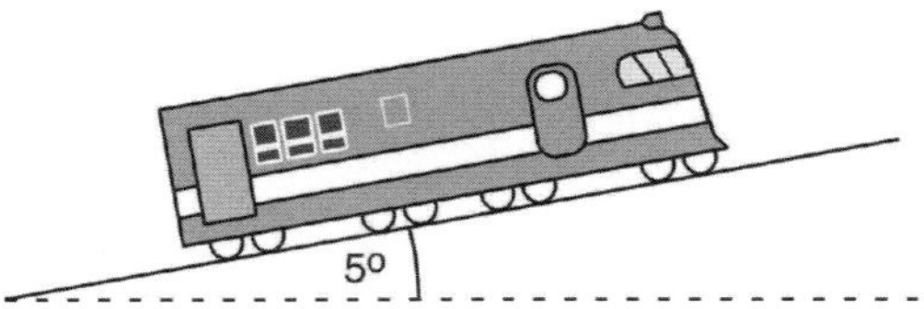

(a) The train reaches the top of the hill at 10 m s^{-1} . What is its kinetic energy?

2 marks

The train coasts down the hill on the other side into a valley.

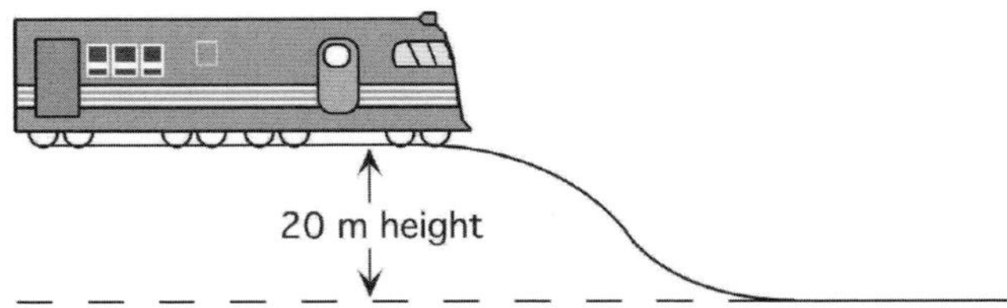

(b) Calculate its speed at the bottom of the hill. Assume there is still no retarding friction.

2 marks

(c) In fact, there was retarding friction (air resistance), and its speed was only 18 m s^{-1}. Calculate the amount of energy transformed into thermal energy.

3 marks

(d) Later, the train travels up another slope very slowly. It gains 4.0 MJ of gravitational PE. The efficiency of its engines is 20%. Calculate the amount of chemical energy transformed from its fuel in climbing the hill.

3 marks

Question 11

A cyclist pushes on her pedals with a force *F*. She doubles her *cadence* (the rate at which the pedals rotate). Due to a tailwind, she does not need to change her force on the pedals. Discuss the effect of this on the rate at which she does work (the power).

3 marks

Question 12

Two cars travelling at 5 m s^{-1} collide head-on and lock together. Straight after the collision the wreckage is travelling *left* at 1.5 m s^{-1}.

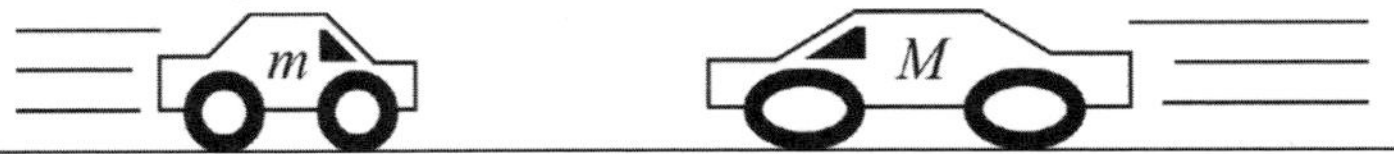

What percentage of the KE before the collision was transformed into other forms of energy during the collision?

3 marks

Question 13

The graph below shows how the stopping distance of a car varies with its speed in good conditions. The car brakes are in good condition.

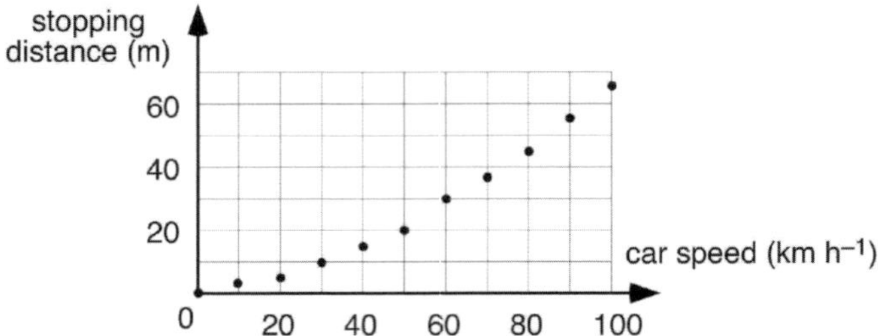

When the speed doubles (e.g. from 40 to 80 km h^{-1}), the stopping distance increases by more than a factor of two. Outline how physics principles apply to this situation.

4 marks

Question 14

Lucia starts to skate along a horizontal bitumen road. The force of rolling friction between her skates and the road is constant at 150 N. The graph below represents the relationship between the driving force that she exerts and her distance from her starting position. She has a mass of 25 kg.

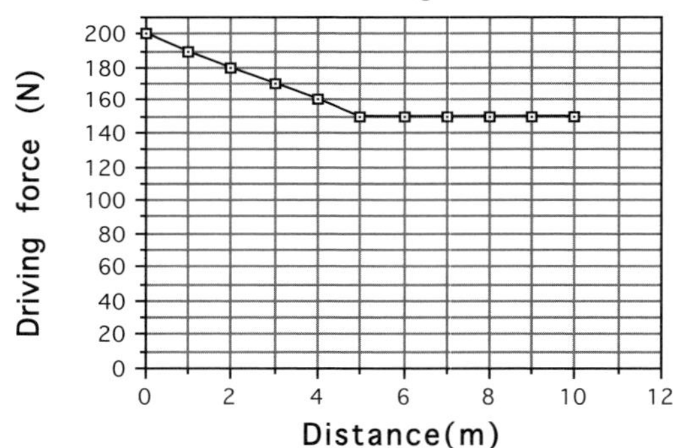

(a) Describe the changes in her speed as she travels 10 m from the starting position. Explain these changes in terms of the forces acting on her.

2 marks

(b) Calculate the work done by Lucia in the first 5.0 m of travel.

2 marks

(c) It takes her 3.0 s to travel the first 5.0 m. What is her average power output?

2 marks

(d) Calculate the work done to oppose the force of rolling friction in this time.

2 marks

(e) What is her final speed by the time she has travelled 10 m?

2 marks

Question 15

Jan slowly climbs a 10 m vertical ladder. She has a mass of 60 kg.

(a) Calculate the increase in Jan's gravitational potential energy during the climb to the top of the ladder.

2 marks

(b) The climb involves the use of 30 kJ of chemical energy from Jan's stores. Calculate the efficiency of energy transfer from chemical potential energy to gravitational potential energy.

2 marks

(c) The climb takes Jan 3.0 minutes. At what rate is Jan using up chemical potential energy?

2 marks

Question 16

Jack is pulling a crate along the floor as shown.

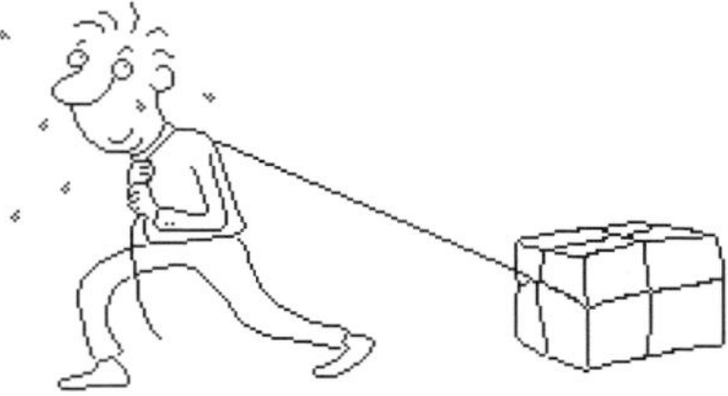

The horizontal component of the force on the crate varies with distance as shown in the graph below.

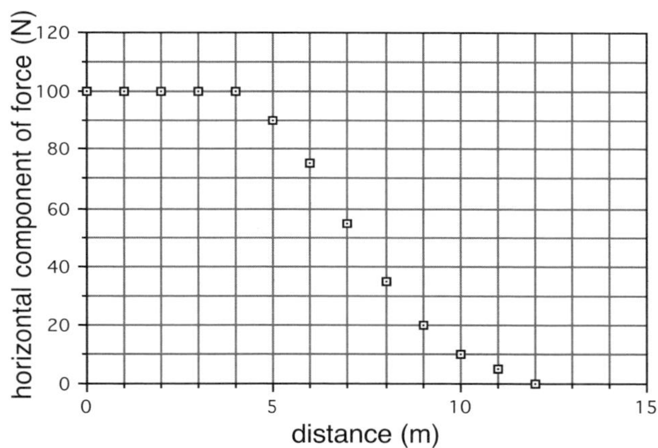

(a) Estimate the work done on the crate by this force as it travels 12 m along the floor.

2 marks

The force exerted by Jack on the rope is greater than the horizontal component shown in the graph. This is due to the angle between the rope and the horizontal. An effect of this is to reduce the friction between the crate and the floor.

(b) Explain carefully why the friction is reduced. Use a labelled diagram showing the forces on the crate in your answer.

3 marks

Question 17

When Iain was six he found he could climb the goal posts at the football oval. This alarmed his parents. One day he climbed 6.0 m high. (He had a mass of 20 kg.)

(a) What was his gravitational potential energy increase during this climb?

2 marks

(b) The climb took Iain 15 seconds. What was the average mechanical power he developed during the climb?

2 marks

(c) On another attempt at this climb, he slipped when he was only 2 m above his dad. Fortunately his dad caught him. How much kinetic energy does his dad absorb from his falling son when he catches him? Ignore friction.

2 marks

Question 18

Brad is driving his car along the freeway.

The net force acting on the car over a 100 m interval is 2000 N.

(a) By how much will the kinetic energy of the car increase over this distance?

2 marks

On another occasion, the car, which has a mass of 1.0 t, is travelling at 36 km/h. It comes to a hill travelling at this speed. The car coasts up the hill, without using the engine or the brakes. Air resistance and rolling friction can be neglected. Some distance up the hill the car stops.

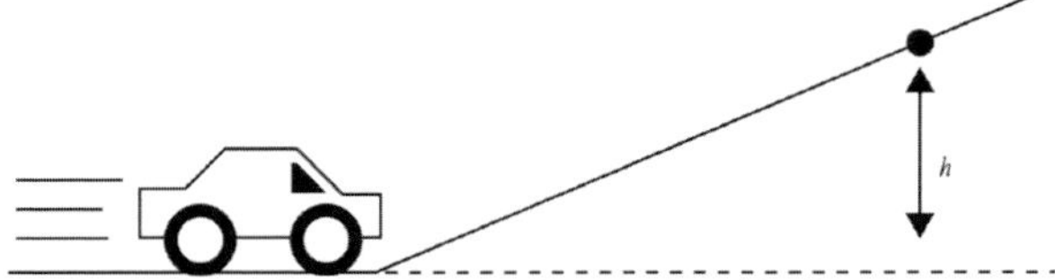

(b) Calculate the height, *h*, that the car has gained before it stops.

3 marks

Question 19

Jim climbs a tall ladder in order to make a bungee jump. The ladder is 65 m high. Jim has a mass of 70 kg.

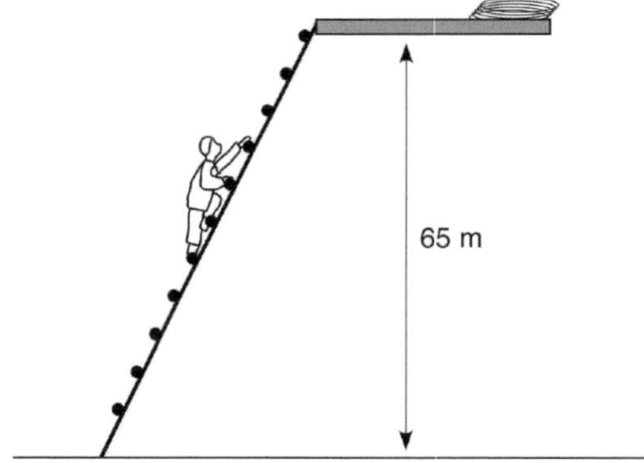

(a) When Jim has reached the top of the ladder, how much gravitational potential energy has he gained? (Give the answer to three significant figures.)

2 marks

(b) If Jim were to step off the platform before fastening himself to the bungee rope (he does not do this), how much kinetic energy would he gain just before he hit the ground? (Ignore air resistance, answer to three significant figures.)

1 mark

(c) Jim fastens himself to the bungee rope before he steps off the platform. The bungee rope stretches, bringing him to a stop exactly 1.0 m from the ground. Calculate how much elastic potential energy is stored in the bungee rope at this point. (Give the answer to three significant figures.)

3 marks

Question 20

Lucy slides down a snow slope on a toboggan. As she does so, gravitational potential energy is converted to other forms of energy, including kinetic energy.

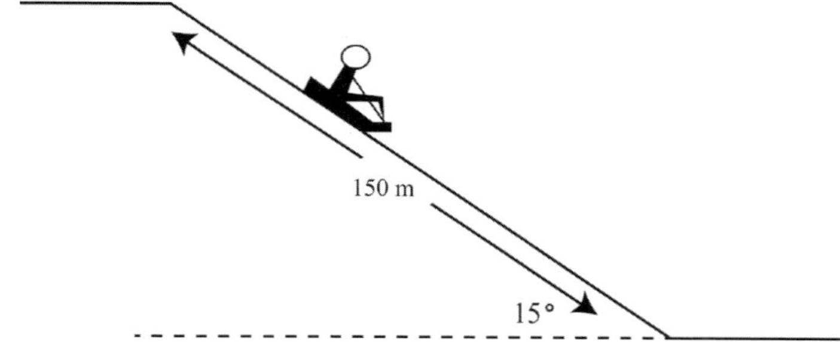

(a) What vertical distance does Lucy move through down the slope?

2 marks

(b) The mass of Lucy and toboggan is 100 kg. Calculate the loss in gravitational potential energy of Lucy and toboggan as they move down the slope.

2 marks

(c) If 30% of Lucy's gravitational potential energy is converted to kinetic energy, what speed is she travelling at the bottom of the slope?

3 marks

(d) If the other 70% of the gravitational potential energy is transferred to the environment by heating due to friction with the slope, calculate the average friction force operating as the toboggan slides down the hill.

2 marks

(e) Calculate the coefficient of friction between the toboggan and the slope.

3 marks

Question 21

Frankie (mass 80 kg) drops 5 m onto a trampoline. When he strikes the trampoline, his speed is 10 m/s. The trampoline stops his motion momentarily. His mass is 80 kg.

(a) Calculate how much work has been done on Frankie by the trampoline in stopping his downward motion.

2 marks

(b) The trampoline then propels Frankie upwards with a speed of 6 m s^{-1}. Calculate the size of the change in his *velocity* during his 'collision' with the trampoline.

2 marks

(c) Calculate how much energy is converted to forms *other than* kinetic energy.

2 marks

Question 22

Jim tries to reduce his weight by eating less and exercising on a bike. When he pedals at 1.2 kW, 25% is converted to mechanical work; the rest is dissipated as heat. How many joules of thermal energy does he produce if he pedals for 8 min.?

2 marks

Question 23

A cyclist travelling at 10 m s^{-1} along a flat concrete track expends 14 W in rolling resistance and 200 W in air resistance.

(a) Calculate the rolling friction force acting on the bicycle.

2 marks

(b) Calculate the air resistance force acting on the bicycle.

2 marks

(c) If the bicycle were to travel up a hill with a gradient of 7° on the same surface at the same speed, calculate the extra force required due to the hill. The combined mass of the cyclist and bicycle is 80 kg.

2 marks

(d) Calculate the mechanical energy from the cyclist riding up the hill in 1.0 min.

2 marks

Question 24

The graph shown below was drawn by a student investigating the stretch of a spring. However, he forgot to add number scales to the axes. He knew that the maximum stretch of the spring was 1.5 m, and at that point the spring stored potential energy of 4500 J.

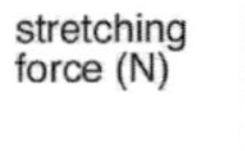

(a) Calculate the force constant of the spring.

2 marks

(b) Label both axes with correct number scales.

4 marks

Chapter 5 – Momentum, energy, simple systems

Question 1

The collision between two 2.0 kg balls can be modelled by two isolated masses colliding.

(a) Which of the following is closest to the speed and direction of the left-hand mass after the collision?

A. 0.5 m s^{-1} to the right
B. 0.5 m s^{-1} to the left
C. 1.5 m s^{-1} to the left
D. 1.5 m s^{-1} to the right

1 mark

(b) Which of the following best describes the kinetic energy before and after the collision?

A. The kinetic energy increases by 1.5 J.
B. The kinetic energy decreases by 1.5 J.
C. The kinetic energy remains constant at 4.0 J.
D. The kinetic energy remains constant at 2.5 J.

1 mark

(c) This collision could best be described as

A. an elastic collision.
B. an inelastic collision.
C. a partially elastic collision.
D. a completely inelastic collision.

1 mark

Question 2

Two cars, each travelling at 5.0 m s^{-1}, are heading towards each other. They collide head on and lock together. One has mass *m* and the other has mass *M.*

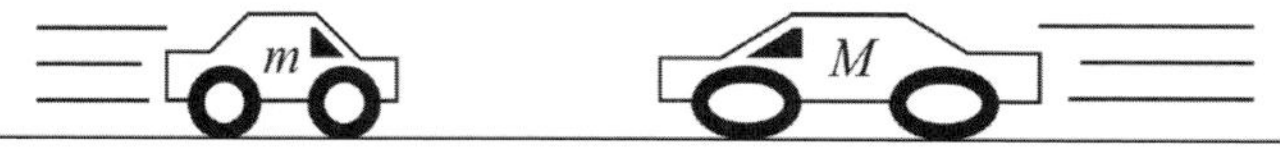

(a) Straight after the collision the wreckage is travelling *left* at 1.5 m s^{-1}. Which of the following is closest to the percentage of the kinetic energy before the collision that is transformed into other forms of energy during the collision?

A. 100%
B. 90%
C. 70%
D. 30%

1 mark

(b) Which of the following is closest to the impulse on the car of mass *m* during the collision?

A. 6.5*m* to the left
B. 6.5*m* to the left
C. 3.5*M* to the right
D. 5.0*m* to the left

1 mark

Question 3

Two skaters are on a surface that has no rolling friction. Malachi (mass 55 kg) approaches Sarah (mass 45 kg) moving at 5.0 m s^{-1}. Sarah is moving in the same direction as Malachi at 1.0 m s^{-1}. They join hands and skate freely in the same direction.

(a) Which of the following is closest to their combined speed after they join hands?

A. 3.2 m s^{-1}
B. 4.0 m s^{-1}
C. 5.0 m s^{-1}
D. 6.0 m s^{-1}

1 mark

(b) Which of the following describes the physics of this 'collision' best?

A. The combined momentum and KE has not changed.
B. The combined KE has remained constant.
C. The combined momentum has remained constant.
D. Both the combined momentum and KE have changed.

1 mark

(c) Without pushing or pulling, Malachi and Sarah let go of each other. Which of the following best describes what happens immediately after they let go?

A. They return to the speeds that they had before.
B. Malachi moves at 0 m s^{-1} and Sarah moves at 5.0 m s^{-1}.
C. Both move at the same speed in the same direction.
D. Both move at the same speed in different directions.

1 mark

Question 4

A car is travelling at 6.0 m s^{-1} when it crashes into two stationary cars. All the cars have the same mass (750 kg). They stick together and travel in the same direction as before. There is very little friction.

(a) Which of the following is closest to their combined speed after the crash?

A. 2.0 m s^{-1}
B. 3.0 m s^{-1}
C. 4.5 m s^{-1}
D. 6.0 m s^{-1}

1 mark

(b) Which of the following is closest to the magnitude of the momentum lost by the car on the left?

A. 150 N s
B. 300 N s
C. 450 N s
D. 600 N s

1 mark

(c) Which of the following is closest to the magnitude of the impulse on the middle car?

A. 150 N s
B. 300 N s
C. 450 N s
D. 600 N s

1 mark

Question 5

Two blocks have a collision on a frictionless surface. The situation before the collision is shown in the diagram.

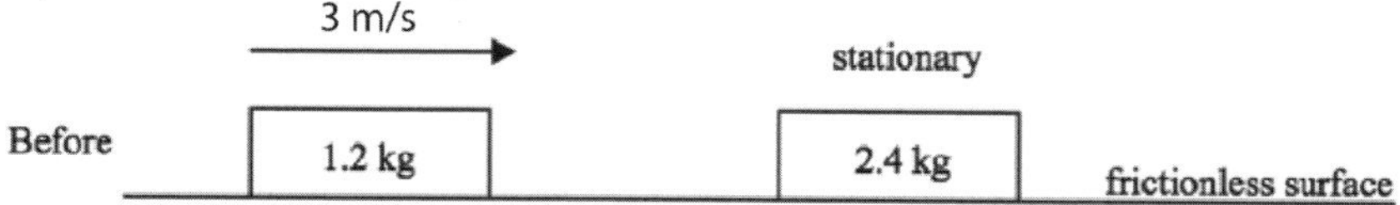

(a) On one occasion, the blocks stick together after the collision, due to a fast acting glue. Their speed after the collision will be closest to

A. 1.0 m s^{-1}
B. 1.2 m s^{-1}
C. 1.5 m s^{-1}
D. 1.8 m s^{-1}

(b) On another occasion, the blocks collide elastically. Which of the following best describes the velocities of the blocks after the collision? (The speed of the 1.2 kg block is written first; the units are m s^{-1}; + means to the right, – means to the left).

A. (+2, +1)
B. (–1, +2)
C. (–1.5, +1.5)
D. (0, +1.5)

2 marks

Question 6

A pole-vaulter falls freely through a vertical height of 4.6 m onto thick foam mats. Just before she hits the mats she has a momentum of 475 N s.

(a) Calculate the mass of the pole-vaulter. Ignore the effects of air resistance.

2 marks

(b) Calculate the kinetic energy (in kJ) of the pole-vaulter just before she hits the mats.

2 marks

(c) After a short time, the pole-vaulter comes to rest on the mats. Explain what has happened to the kinetic energy and momentum that she had just before she hit the mats.

2 marks

Question 7

A stationary golf ball (mass = 57 g) is struck by a golf club. The average force that the golf club exerts on the ball is 45 N, for a time of 35 ms. Calculate the speed of the ball as it leaves the face of the golf club.

2 marks

Question 8

A basketball is bounced vertically on a floor, striking the floor at 8 m s^{-1}, and rebounding at 6 m s^{-1}. Its mass is 400 g. The collision lasts 80 ms.

(a) Calculate the size and direction of the velocity change of the ball during the bounce.

3 marks

(b) Calculate the magnitude of the impulse of the net force on the ball during the bounce.

2 marks

(c) Calculate the size of the average net force exerted on the ball during the bounce.

2 marks

(d) Describe the momentum transfers that occur during the collision of the ball with the floor.

2 marks

Question 9

A bag of sand is dropped from a window. Just before it strikes the ground it has a momentum of 1000 N s. It hits the ground without bouncing. If momentum is always conserved, explain what has happened to the 1000 N s it had before the collision.

2 marks

Question 10

In a car, the driver's head (m = 7.0 kg) collides horizontally with an airbag at 8.0 m s^{-1}. The driver's head comes to rest in 0.16 s. This can be modelled as a collision between the head and the airbag.

(a) Calculate the magnitude of the impulse that the airbag exerts on the driver's head during this collision.

2 marks

(b) Compare the impulse that the airbag exerts on the driver's head with the impulse that the driver's head exerts on the airbag.

2 marks

Question 11

Airbags in motor cars are designed to lengthen the time of collisions of people with parts of the car during accidents. Explain why lengthening the time of collisions should lead to less injuries to people in motor car accidents.

3 marks

Question 12

Read the following passage.

In a road crash, there are really two collisions. The first is when the car hits something and stops. The part of the vehicle that receives the hit first stops abruptly. The passenger compartment stops more slowly as some of the impact is absorbed in the crushing of the engine bay. The result is that the passenger compartment often remains relatively undamaged. The more important collision is when an occupant hits part of the car. Unrestrained occupants keep moving inside the passenger compartment while the car comes to a stop. They are still moving forward at their original speed when they hit the steering wheel, windscreen or some other part of the car.

The second collision is the more important collision because most injuries are caused by it. Explain why. Refer to the *time* that each collision lasts in your answer.

3 marks

Question 13

Justify why a 'crumple zone' at the front of a passenger car is effective in reducing the likelihood of injuries in a head-on collision.

3 marks

Question 14

A car of mass 1000 kg collides head-on with a smaller car of mass 500 kg. Before the collision the smaller car was travelling at 5 m s^{-1}. Immediately after the collision the two cars are stationary. The collision takes a total time of 1.0 s.

(a) Calculate the speed of the larger car immediately before the collision.

3 marks

(b) Passengers in both cars are firmly restrained, so that they slow down at the same rate as the vehicles. Compare the decelerations of passengers in the two cars, and any safety implications.

4 marks

Question 15

The braking distance of a 100 kg car travelling at 8.0 m s^{-1} is 10 m, without skidding. At higher speeds, the car uses exactly the same braking force. Calculate the stopping distance when the car is travelling at 20 m s^{-1}.

Question 16

In 2011 the NSW government doubled demerit points for speeding. One justification for this action is that it leads to a large reduction in stopping distances of vehicles. Take the case of a 500 kg car travelling at 50 km h^{-1}. At this speed, this car can stop in 14 m. Calculate the stopping distance of this car if it is only travelling at 45 km h^{-1} (a 10% reduction in speed). Assume the braking force is the same at both speeds.

4 marks

Question 17

A 500 kg car collides with a safety spring barrier at the end of a road.

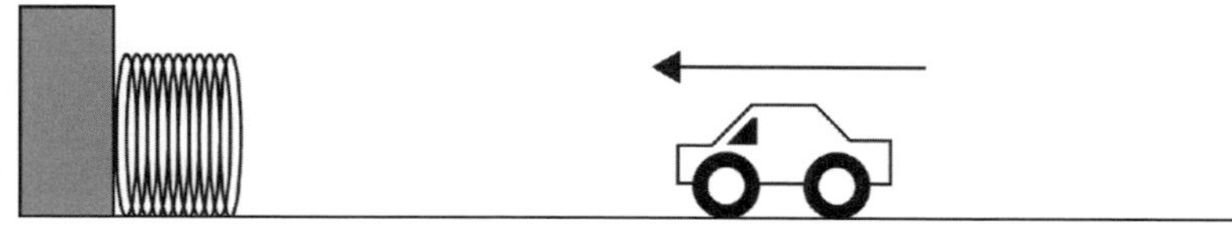

The spring compresses, and after 0.50 s, the car stops momentarily. The average force exerted by the spring on the car during this time is 15 kN.

(a) Calculate the initial speed of the car when it first contacts the spring.

2 marks

After the car comes to a stop, the spring pushes the car backwards so that it ends up travelling at the same speed as before, in the opposite direction.

(b) Discuss the transformations of energy that occur in this process.

3 marks

(c) Outline the transfers of momentum that take place during this process.

3 marks

Question 18

Two small disc shaped objects ('pucks') collide on an air table, where friction can be ignored. The diagrams below show the pucks before and after the collision. The dashed line shows the direction of the left-hand puck before the collision. The other puck is at rest. They have the same mass (100 g).

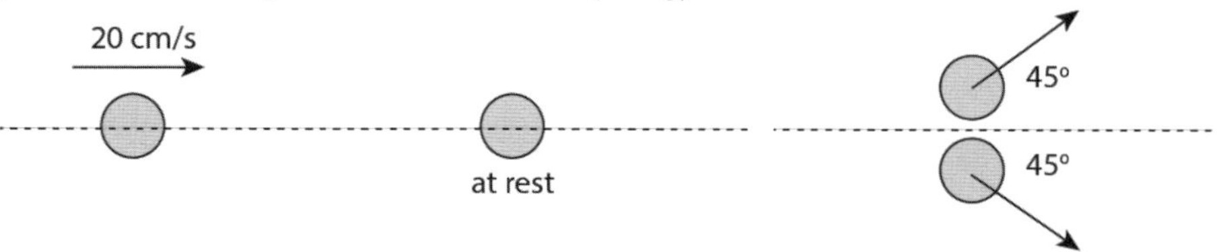

before the collision *after the collision*

After the collision both pucks move off at 45° to the original direction of the left-hand puck. They are travelling at the same speed, v.

(a) Use conservation of momentum to determine the value of v.

3 marks

(b) Determine, using calculations, whether the collision is elastic or inelastic.

3 marks

(c) Compare the impulse that each puck exerts on the other. Show your reasoning.

3 marks

Question 19

Two 1.0 kg balls (A and B) are dropped from a height of 10 m onto a hard, concrete floor. Ball A rebounds at 14 m s^{-1}; ball B does not rebound at all (it is made of 'blutak'). Ignore the effects of air resistance.

(a) Classify these collisions as elastic or inelastic. Use calculations.

3 marks

(b) Calculate the change in velocity of each ball, giving magnitude and direction.

4 marks

(c) Both collisions last for 250 ms. Calculate the average force that each ball exerts on the floor during the collisions.

4 marks

Question 20

Recently a 90 kg skydiver was reported jumping out of a plane without a parachute at a height of over 7500 m, landing safely in a net. He was moving at about 55 m s^{-1} just before he reached the net. The action of the net can be modelled as a device which exerts a constant upward force of 4410 N. When the skydiver stops, the net exerts a further force equal to his weight.

(a) Calculate the distance that this model net would take to bring the skydiver to rest.

2 marks

(b) Calculate the impulse that the model net would exert on the skydiver.

2 marks

(c) Explain what happens to the vertical momentum of the skydiver from the time he steps out of the plane to the time he comes to rest in the net. Refer to the principle of momentum conservation. Ignore air resistance effects.

4 marks

Question 21

The diagram below shows two cars both travelling at 10 m s^{-1} towards a 'blind' corner. The 750 kg car is travelling North and the 1000 kg car West.

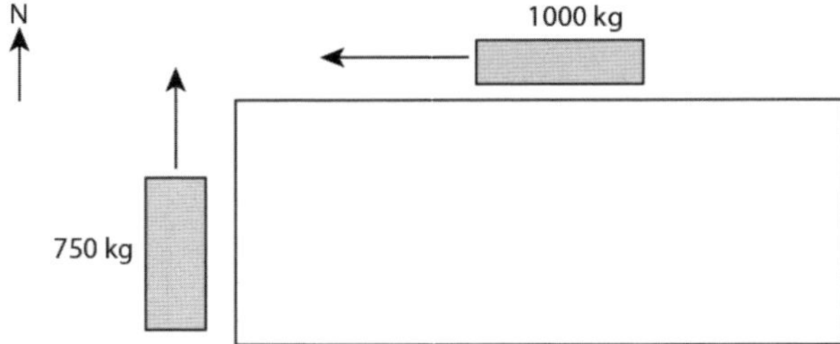

Unfortunately, they crash (no-one is injured) and the cars stick together and slide off in a direction between North and West.

(a) State the components (N and W) of the combined momentum immediately after the crash.

3 marks

(b) Calculate the magnitude of the combined momentum immediately after the crash.

2 marks

(c) Calculate the direction of the combined momentum immediately after the crash as the clockwise angle from the West.

2 marks

(d) Use calculations to determine whether this collision is elastic or inelastic. If it is inelastic, calculate the amount of energy 'lost'.

3 marks

Chapter 6 – Wave properties

Question 1
Explain why a mechanical wave needs a medium.

2 marks

Question 2
Which *one or more* of the following statements are accurate description(s) of the difference between transverse and longitudinal waves?

A. The vibrations of a transverse wave are parallel to the velocity of the wave.
B. The vibrations of a transverse wave are perpendicular to the velocity of the wave.
C. The vibrations of a longitudinal wave are parallel to the velocity of the wave.
D. The vibrations of a longitudinal wave are perpendicular to the velocity of the wave.

1 mark

Question 3
Calculate the wavelength of the sound that some orchestras tune to (A = 440 Hz). (Take the speed of sound as 340 m s^{-1}.)

2 marks

Question 4
Calculate the frequency of microwave radiation of wavelength 2.5 cm.

2 marks

Question 5
Calculate the speed of a tsunami in deep water that has a wavelength of 2.0×10^5 m and a frequency of 1.0×10^{-3} Hz.

2 marks

Question 6
Waves can travel in one, two or three dimensions, depending on their type. In the table below, various kinds of waves are listed. Predict the number of dimensions that the different waves can travel in (1, 2 or 3) by placing the number 1, 2 or 3 beside each wave type.

Sound waves	
Waves in a guitar string	
Ripples in a pond	
Waves on the surface of a drum	

4 marks

Question 7
Compare *longitudinal* and *transverse* waves, using an example of one of each kind.

4 marks

Question 8
At large public events (where they are not banned) 'Mexican' waves can be sometimes seen in the crowd. Describe, preferably with a diagram, the following:

(a) the nature of the 'particles' of the medium
(b) the direction of 'particle' motion – transverse or longitudinal
(c) the 'wavelength' of such waves
(d) the period of such waves
(e) the speed of such waves

5 marks

Question 9

Which of the following is particularly associated with *wave motion*?

A. The transfer of energy from one place to another.
B. The transfer of matter from one place to another.
C. Vibrations which transfer energy from one place to another.
D. Vibrations which are transverse to the direction of motion.

1 mark

Question 10

Water waves in deep water can be modelled quite well by sinusoidal transverse waves. Describe the movement of water particles in such a wave.

2 marks

Question 11

The sketch below shows a side-on view of a wave in a rope. It is a *travelling* wave, and is moving from the left to the right.

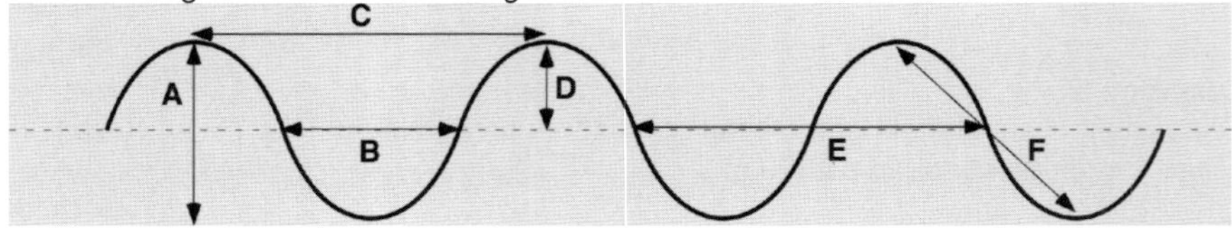

(a) Identify *one or more* of the arrows labelled A to F that best describes the size of the *amplitude* of the wave shown.

1 mark

(b) Identify *one or more* of the arrows labelled A to F that best describes the size of the *wavelength* of the wave shown.

1 mark

(c) Which of the following statements best describes the *frequency* of the wave?

A. The frequency of the wave is related to the time it takes a wave to travel any fixed distance.
B. The frequency of the wave is related to the time it takes a wave crest to travel one wavelength.
C. The frequency of the wave is inversely related to the time it takes a wave to travel one wavelength.
D. The frequency of the wave is equal to the time it takes a wave crest to travel one wavelength.

1 mark

Question 12

The graph below shows a snapshot of a transverse travelling wave at time $t = 0$ s.

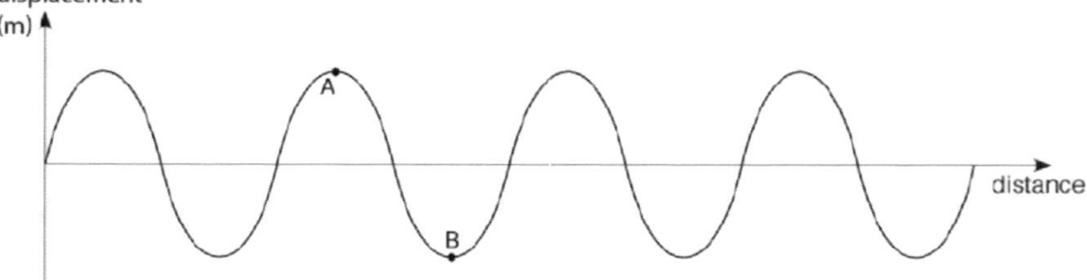

(a) The vertical distance between points A and B is equal to 2.6 m. The horizontal distance between points A and B is 4.0 m. Calculate the value of the *amplitude* and the *wavelength* of the wave shown above.

2 marks

(b) A snapshot is taken of the wave at a time t = 24 s. The snapshot shows the wave in *exactly the same position* as in the diagram on the previous page. Which *one* of the values below *could* be a measure of the *period* of the transverse wave?

A. 12 s
B. 18 s
C. 36 s
D. 48 s

2 marks

(c) Use your previous answers to calculate the speed of the wave.

2 marks

Question 13

A sketch of the wavefronts of a longitudinal wave is shown below. The wave is travelling to the *right*.

(a) Identify any letter(s) in the diagram that identify the position of a *compression*.

2 marks

(b) Identify the letter(s) in the diagram above that identify the position of a *rarefaction*.

2 marks

Question 14

Propose an example of a *longitudinal* wave. Describe how it transfers energy from one place to another. Analyse the movement of any particles associated with the wave.

3 marks

Question 15

The term *amplitude* is used to describe an aspect of wave motion. Recall a wave motion that you are familiar with and describe what is meant by the term.

3 marks

Question 16

When light from the Sun arrives at the surface of the Earth, it warms up surfaces that it falls on. The best explanation for this is that:

A. light particles have travelled from the surface of the Sun to the surface of the Earth; however, these particles transfer no energy.
B. light waves have managed to cross the nearly empty space between the Earth and the Sun by vibrating the few particles that exist between the Earth and the Sun.
C. light waves carry energy from the surface of the Sun to the surface of the Earth; they do not need a medium for transmission.
D. light from the Sun does not warm the surface of the Earth; the warming effect is from other mechanisms.

1 mark

Question 17

Calculate the *wavelength* of the radiation emitted by the radio station *The Edge 96.1* (96.1 MHz). Take the speed of light as 3.0×10^{8} m s^{-1}.

2 marks

Question 18

Calculate the *angular wavenumber (k)* for a wave that has a wavelength of 600 nm. Give your answer in rad.m^{-1}.

2 marks

Question 19
Identify a transverse wave type that is used in everyday life to transfer energy from one point to another. Outline how the energy is transferred from one point to another using this type of transverse wave.

3 marks

Question 20
Identify a longitudinal wave type that is used in everyday life to transfer information from one point to another. Outline how the energy is transferred from one point to another using this type of longitudinal wave.

3 marks

Question 21
Identify the medium involved in the propagation of the following.

(a) tsunami waves
(b) sound waves
(c) earthquake waves

3 marks

Question 22
Students carry out a first-hand investigation of transverse waves travelling along a string. They collect measures of frequency and wavelength, as shown in the table.

wavelength (cm)	*frequency (Hz)*
21	36
33	23
39	20
47	15
59	12
71	11

They plot the data as shown below.

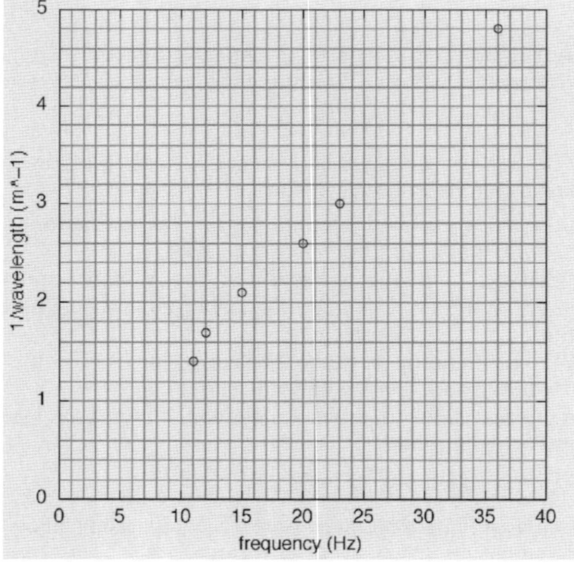

(a) Draw a line of best fit through the plotted points.

2 marks

(b) Use the gradient of the graph to find the speed of the transverse waves.

2 marks

(c) Discuss the advantages of plotting the data in the form shown on the previous page, rather than a simple graph of frequency against wavelength.

2 marks

Question 23

Waves in the ocean often occur in *sets*. One set is sketched below. Surfers often describe the *size* of the waves by the vertical arrow shown in the diagram.

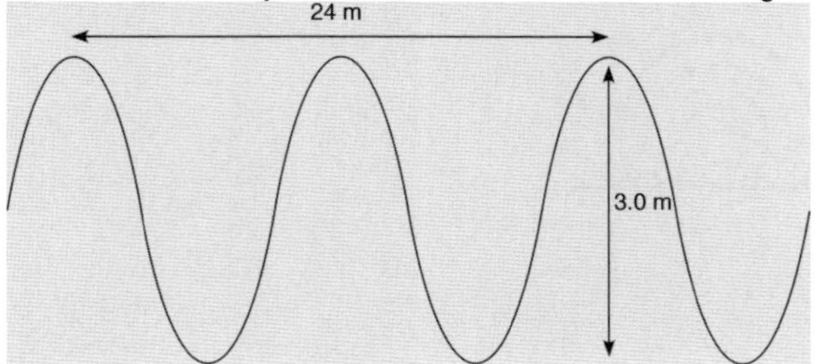

(a) Calculate the amplitude of these waves.

1 mark

(b) Calculate the wavelength of these waves.

1 mark

(c) A surfer measures the time for the wave to travel the 24 m shown in the diagram as 15 seconds. Calculate the frequency of these waves.

2 marks

(d) Calculate the speed of these waves.

2 marks

(e) A little later, another set of three waves arrives. In these waves, the distance from crest to trough is measured as 2.0 m, but they have the same wavelength. Predict whether this set carries more or less energy than the previous set of waves. Justify your answer clearly.

3 marks

Chapter 7 – Wave behaviour

Question 1

The diagrams below show various wave patterns.

A

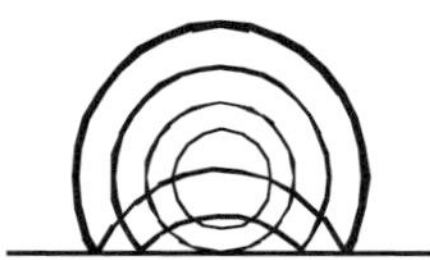

B

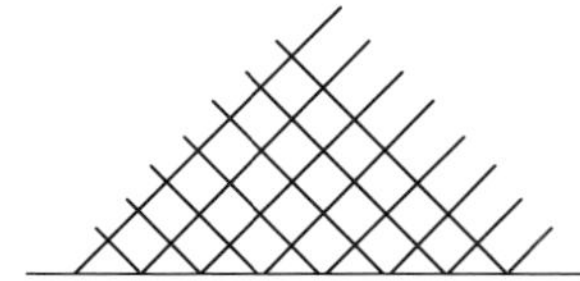

C

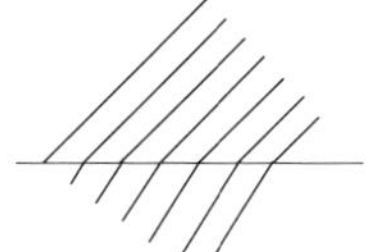

D

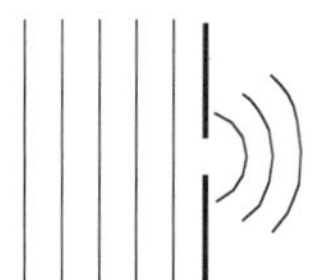

(a) Which *one or more* of the diagrams best shows *reflection* of light using a wave description?

1 mark

(b) Which *one or more* of the diagrams best shows *refraction* of light using a wave description?

1 mark

(c) Which *one or more* of the diagrams best shows *diffraction* of light using a wave description?

1 mark

Question 2

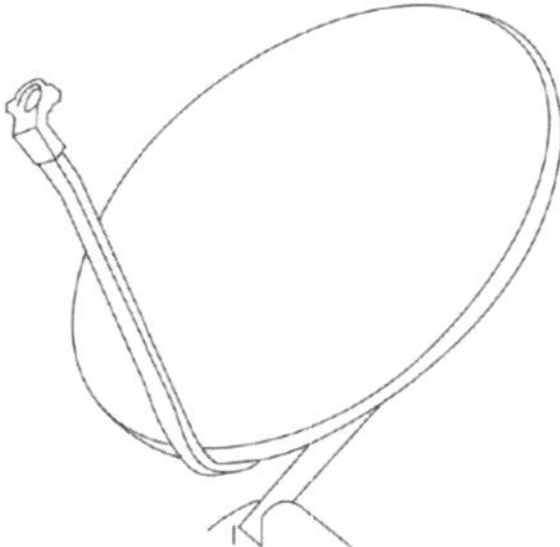

A household TV satellite dish works on the principle of

A. reflection of waves.
B. refraction of waves.
C. diffraction of waves.
D. superposition of waves.

1 mark

Question 3

Foghorns on ships work on the principle of

A. reflection of waves.
B. refraction of waves.
C. diffraction of waves.
D. superposition of waves.

1 mark

Question 4

Noise-cancelling headphones work on the principle of

A. reflection of waves.
B. refraction of waves.
C. diffraction of waves.
D. superposition of waves.

1 mark

Question 5

A surfer catches a wave and surfs towards the shore. Such a wave is an example of

A. a progressive wave.
B. a standing wave.
C. resonance.
D. diffraction.

1 mark

Question 6

A child pushed on a swing goes higher and higher with each push. This is an example of

A. a progressive wave.
B. a standing wave.
C. resonance.
D. diffraction.

1 mark

Question 7

In the diagram below, wavefronts are approaching a *plane* reflecting surface.

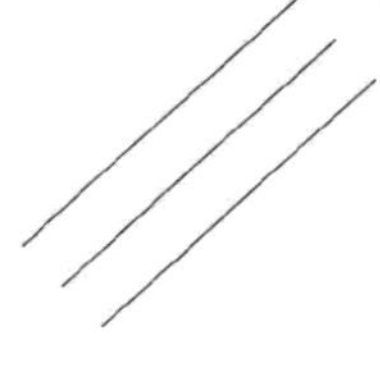

plane reflecting surface

(a) Complete the diagram, showing the subsequent path of the wavefronts until they have all been reflected by the surface.

3 marks

(b) Redraw the diagram in the previous question as a *ray* diagram.

2 marks

Question 8

In the diagram below, wavefronts are approaching a *convex* reflecting surface.

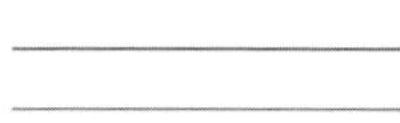

convex reflecting surface

(a) Complete the diagram, showing the subsequent path of the wavefronts until they have all been reflected by the surface.

3 marks

(b) Redraw the diagram in the previous question as a *ray* diagram.

2 marks

Question 9

In the diagram below, wavefronts are approaching a *concave* reflecting surface.

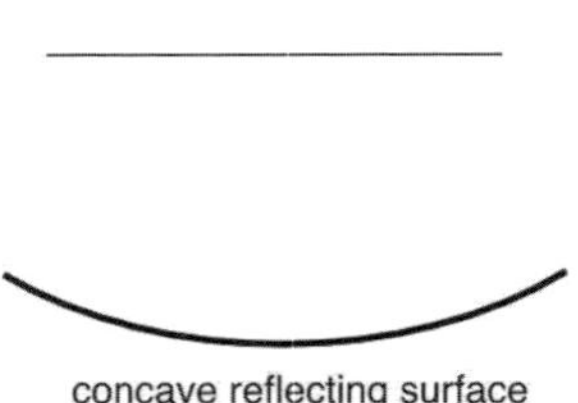

concave reflecting surface

(a) Complete the diagram, showing the subsequent path of the wavefronts until they have all been reflected by the surface.

3 marks

(b) Redraw the diagram in the previous question as a *ray* diagram.

2 marks

Question 10

A beam of light in water approaches the interface between water and the air. Three *wavefronts* are shown in the diagram. They are travelling towards the water-air interface.

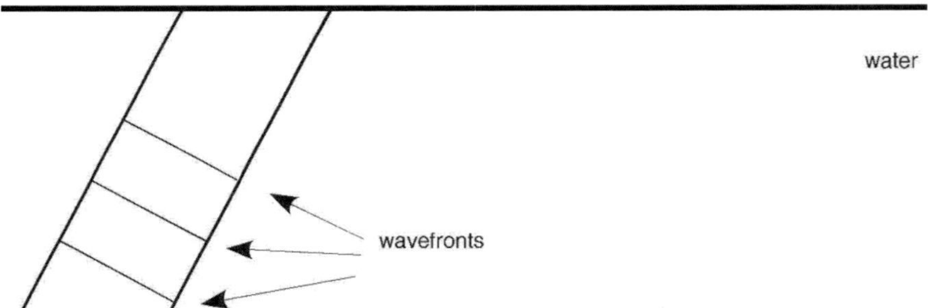

Complete the diagram, showing all the wavefronts in water and at least three complete refracted wavefronts in air. (Do not draw reflected wavefronts.)

4 marks

Question 11

The diagram shows water waves going through a small gap.

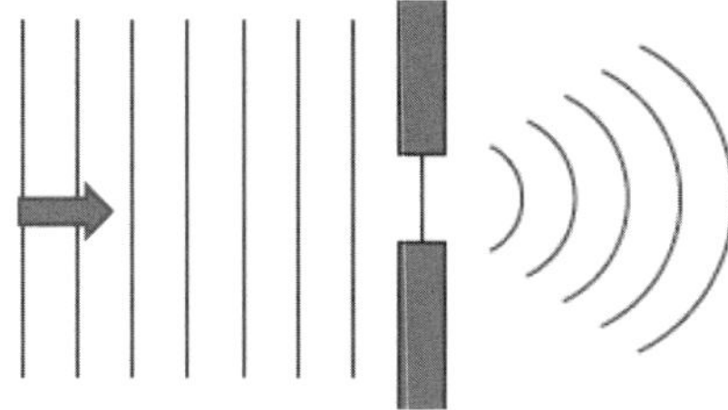

Name this phenomenon and explain how the pattern on the right-hand side is created.

3 marks

Question 12

When ocean waves get closer to the shore of a beach, they enter shallower water, and their speed decreases. The sketch below shows some waves in deep water approaching a beach. The region of shallow water is shown below.

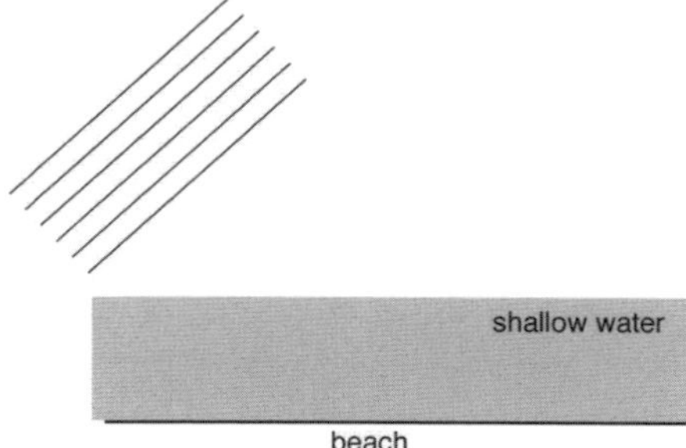

Describe and explain what happens to the waves when they enter the shallow water. You can assume that the speed is constant in the deep water, and also constant (although less) in the shallow water. Analyse the direction, frequency and wavelength of the waves.

4 marks

Question 13

Two pulses of equal wavelength and amplitude are travelling towards each other at 4.0 m s^{-1} as shown below. The distance between the middle of the two pulses is 2.0 m.

(a) Draw the two pulses 0.5 s later.

2 marks

(b) Draw the two pulses 1.0 s later.

2 marks

Question 14

Two pulses of equal wavelength and amplitude are travelling towards each other at 4.0 m s^{-1} as shown below. The distance between the middle of the two pulses is 2.0 m.

(a) Draw the two pulses 0.5 s later.

2 marks

(b) Draw the two pulses 1.0 s later.

2 marks

Question 15

Two wave diagrams are shown below labelled **X** (upper) and **Y** (lower).

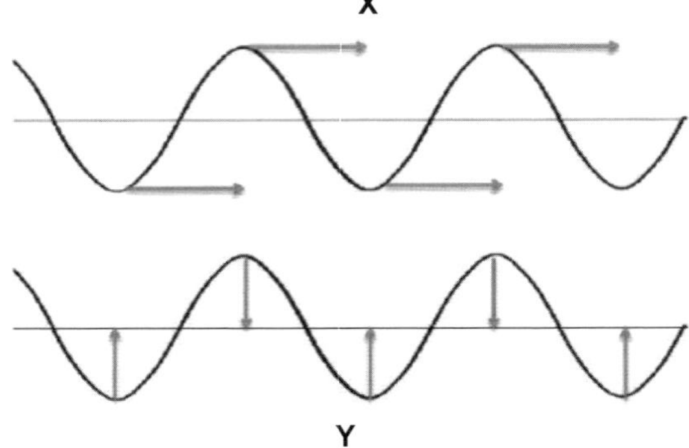

(a) Indicate which wave diagram shows a progressive wave.

1 mark

(b) Indicate which wave diagram shows a standing wave.

1 mark

(c) Using a dotted line draw what wave diagram X would look like one quarter of a period (*T*/4) later than shown above. Give reasons for your answer.

3 marks

(d) Using a dotted line draw what wave diagram Y would look like one quarter of a period (*T*/4) later than shown above. Explain your answer.

3 marks

Question 16

Explain each of the following terms and the relationships between them in a system exhibiting resonance (e.g. a child on a swing being pushed by a parent).

(a) Driving frequency

3 marks

(b) Natural frequency of the oscillating system

3 marks

(c) Amplitude of motion

3 marks

(d) Transformation of energy within the system

3 marks

Question 17

Read the following account of the collapse of the *Angers Suspension Bridge*.

Angers Bridge was a 102 m long suspension bridge in Angers, France. The bridge collapsed in 1850, when 483 French soldiers were marching across it. 226 soldiers died. The bridge was oscillating due to high winds when they were crossing. Although told to 'break step' and space themselves further apart they inadvertently matched their movements to the swaying bridge to stay upright. This increased the oscillation amplitude until the bridge collapsed.

(a) Why had the French soldiers been told to 'break step' and space themselves further apart than normal when crossing the bridge?

3 marks

(b) What were the two driving forces of the oscillations in the bridge?

2 marks

(c) What energy transfers occurred in this system?

2 marks

Question 18

Two physics students do an experiment to explore resonance by blowing horizontally across the top of three bottles as shown below. The first bottle is empty, the second half full of water and the third three quarters full of water. A smartphone audio spectrum analyzer allows the students to determine the frequency of the notes produced.

(a) Explain how an empty bottle resonates when a student blows horizontally across its top.

3 marks

The resonant frequency of the empty bottle is measured as being 120 Hz.

(b) What would the predicted resonant frequencies be for the bottle that is half full of water and the bottle that is three quarters full of water?

2 marks

(c) Explain how you determined the predicted resonant frequencies for the bottle that is half full of water and the bottle that is three quarters full of water.

3 marks

Chapter 8 – Sound waves

Question 1

How are sound waves like ripples in a pond?

A. They both travel at the same speed.
B. They both radiate outward from a central point.
C. They both have the same wavelength.
D. They both have the same frequency.

1 mark

Question 2

The unit used to measure the frequency of sound is the

A. metre.
B. decibel.
C. second.
D. hertz.

1 mark

Question 3

How is the frequency of sound related to its pitch?

A. The higher the frequency of the sound the higher the pitch.
B. The higher the frequency of the sound the lower the pitch.
C. The lower the frequency of the sound the higher the pitch.
D. There is no relationship between the frequency of the sound and the pitch.

1 mark

Question 4

The strengthening of a sound wave when it combines with an object's natural vibration frequency is called

A. refraction.
B. resonance.
C. refraction.
D. diffraction.

1 mark

Question 5

A point source of sound has an intensity of I_0 at a distance of 1.0 m from the source. What will the intensity be at 0.5 m from the source?

A. $4I_0$
B. $2I_0$
C. I_0
D. $I_0/2$

1 mark

Question 6

Which of the following best describes how a loudspeaker makes sound waves?

A. The loudspeaker cone vibrates back and forth at close to the speed of sound.
B. The loudspeaker cone causes electromagnetic vibrations in the air.
C. The loudspeaker cone vibrates from side to side causing transverse vibrations.
D. The loudspeaker cone adds back and forth vibration to the air particles' thermal motion.

1 mark

Question 7

A small candle is placed in front of a loudspeaker that emits a single frequency sound.

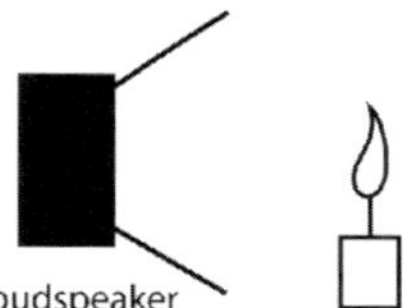

(a) As the loudspeaker produces sound, the candle flame

A. remains stationary.
B. vibrates vertically.
C. moves steadily to the right.
D. vibrates horizontally.

1 mark

(b) This demonstrates that sound is

A. an acoustic wave.
B. a longitudinal wave.
C. a transverse wave.
D. a surface wave.

1 mark

Question 8

When a sound from a musical instrument is described as becoming 'louder and lower in pitch', this means that

A. the amplitude of the pressure variations has increased and the frequency has also increased.
B. the amplitude of the pressure variations has decreased and the frequency has also decreased.
C. the amplitude of the pressure variations has decreased and the frequency has increased.
D. the amplitude of the pressure variations has increased and the frequency has decreased.

1 mark

Question 9

A 60 cm long guitar string is fixed at both ends as shown.

(a) Sketch the first, second and third harmonics for notes generated on the guitar string.

3 marks

(b) Calculate the wavelength of the first harmonic.

1 mark

(c) If the fundamental frequency of the guitar string is $\boldsymbol{f_0}$, what will be the frequency of the third harmonic?

1 mark

Question 10

A sound barrier is constructed on the side of a new freeway to reduce sound levels heard at the nearby houses. A straight line from the car's engine to the top of the barrier passes over the top of the nearby houses. Sound is generated by the tyres and engines of vehicles.

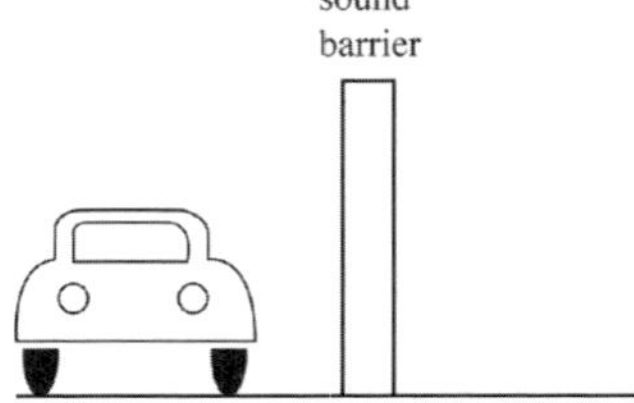

(a) Explain how reflection lessens the sound level heard at the houses.

2 marks

(b) Explain how sound can still be heard at the houses due to diffraction.

2 marks

Question 11

A sketch of a simple pipe open at both ends is shown below. The fundamental frequency of the pipe is 668 Hz. The length of the pipe is ***L***. Take the speed of sound as 334 m s^{-1}.

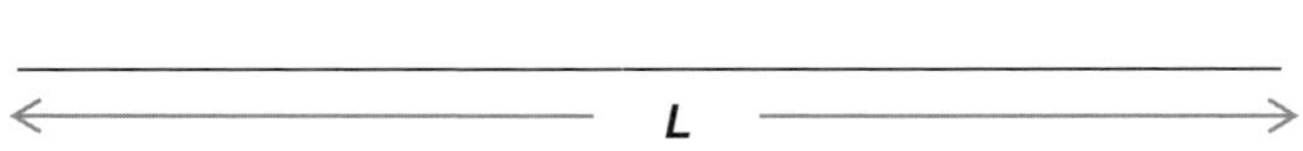

(a) Calculate the wavelength of the 668 Hz note.

1 mark

(b) Calculate the length of the pipe ***L***.

2 marks

(c) Calculate the frequency of the second harmonic for the pipe.

1 mark

(d) Explain why this pipe cannot produce a resonant frequency at 334 Hz.

2 marks

Question 12

The sound intensity ***I*** is measured as being 0.40 W m^{-2} at a distance of 2.00 m from a point source of sound.

(a) Calculate the sound intensity at a distance 3.00 m from the same point sound source.

2 marks

(b) At what distance from the same point sound source would the sound be measured as having an intensity 0.04 W m^{-2}?

2 marks

Question 13

The graph below is a graph of the pressure variation caused by a sound wave travelling through air, as a function of time, measured at a stationary point.

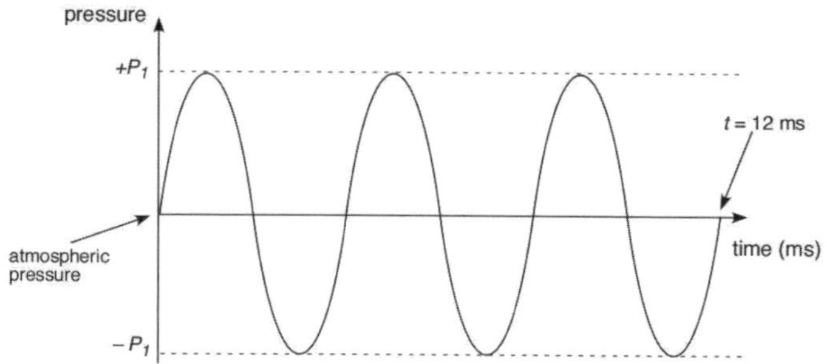

(a) From the information in the graph, state the number of *rarefactions* present in the 12 ms time interval shown.

1 mark

(b) From the information in the graph, state the period of the sound wave.

1 mark

(c) Use the information in the graph to calculate the frequency of this sound wave.

2 marks

(d) The speed of sound of the wave when the graph data was obtained was 335 m s^{-1}. Use this and the information in the graph above to calculate the *wavelength* of the sound wave.

2 marks

(e) Which of the following best represents the *amplitude* of the sound wave in the graph?

A. *P*1
B. $-P_1$
C. $2P_1$
D. $-2P_1$

1 mark

Question 14

The graph below shows the pressure variation of a sound wave at a point in time, graphed against distance from the source of the wave.

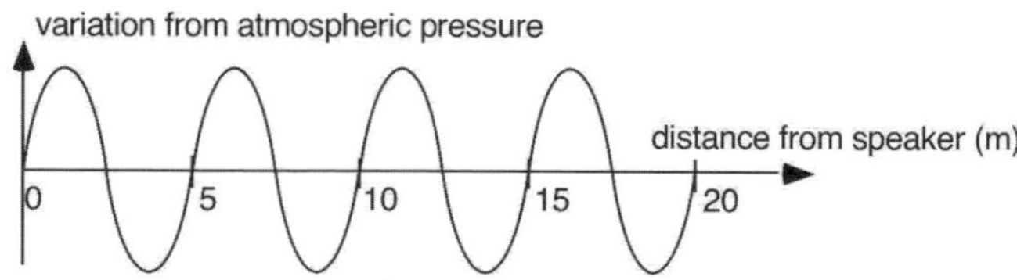

The speed of sound is 343 m s^{-1}. Calculate the frequency of the wave shown in the graph.

2 marks

Question 15

On the graph grid below, sketch the graph of a sinusoidal sound wave as a pressure variation against time, with the following properties:

- three full cycles of the wave
- frequency of 500 Hz
- maximum pressure variation from atmospheric pressure of 10^2 Pa (N m^{-2})

Label the axes carefully.

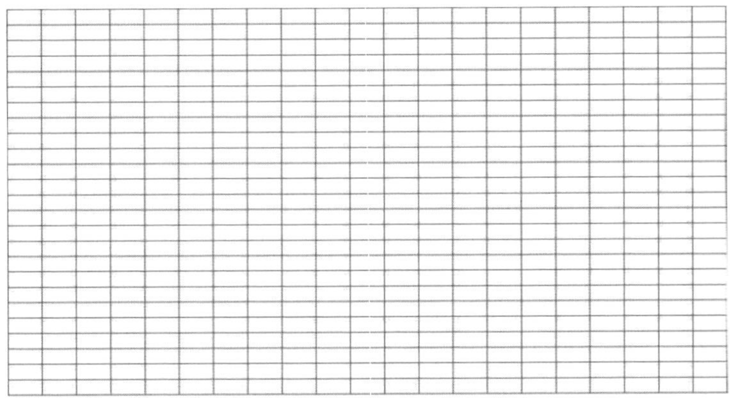

4 marks

Question 16

The seven images in the diagram below illustrate a fundamental property of waves.

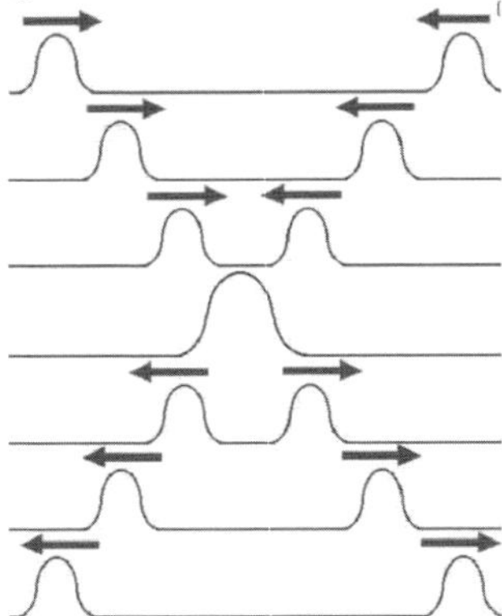

Identify this fundamental property, and use it to explain how the *fourth* image is formed.

3 marks

Question 17

Pressure–time graphs are shown below for two sound waves, A and B.

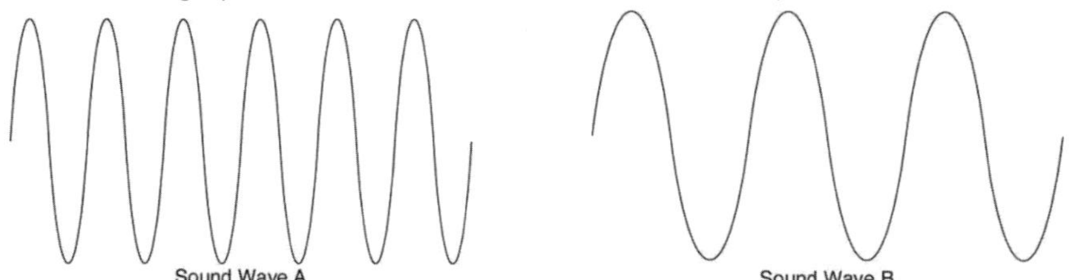

Both sound waves (as shown) start and finish at the same time. Carefully sketch the resulting sound wave when they overlap at the same point in space.

4 marks

Question 18

A student has sketched the pressure variation with time for three sound waves. Two of them overlap to form the third wave. He cannot remember which two combine to form the third wave. Identify which is the *resultant* wave; A, B or C. Justify your conclusion.

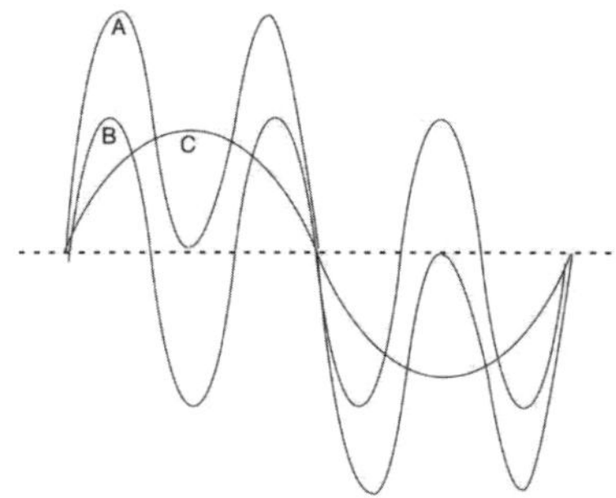

3 marks

Question 19

A jet plane flying to the right at 864 km h^{-1} creates a pattern of sound waves as shown. Take the speed of sound as 1080 km h^{-1}. Stationary 'observers' are at positions X and Y. The main frequency of the sound emitted by the jet engine is 2.00 kHz.

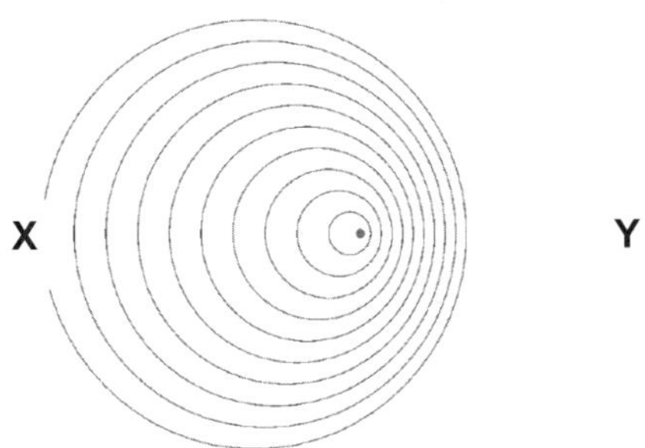

(a) Calculate the speed of the jet in m s^{-1}.

1 mark

(b) Calculate the speed of sound at the jet's altitude in m s^{-1}.

1 mark

(c) Would an observer at position X hear a lower, the same or a higher frequency than that produced by the jet engine? Give reasons.

2 marks

(d) Calculate the frequency that an observer at position Y would hear.

2 marks

(e) Calculate the frequency that an observer at position Y would hear if the observer at Y was moving at a speed of 432 km h^{-1} to the *left*.

2 marks

(f) What speed would an observer at X need to travel to hear the original 2.00 kHz sound emitted by the jet engine. Give reasons.

2 marks

Question 20

Two identical 256 Hz tuning forks are placed next to each other.

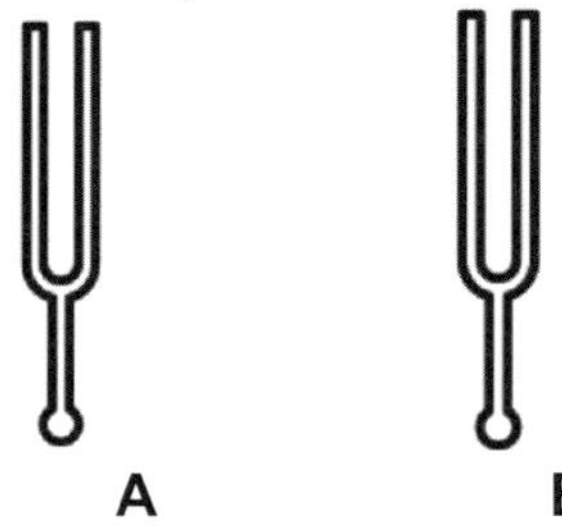

(a) Explain what will happen to the tuning fork on the right (**B**) if the one on the left (**A**) is struck and vibrates giving a sound of frequency 256 Hz.

2 marks

(b) Two identical small pieces of 'Blu Tack' are added to each of the prongs of the tuning fork on the right (**B**).

(i) When the tuning fork on the right (**B**) is struck, will the note produced by **B** be of a higher, the same or a lower frequency than 256 Hz? Give reasons.

2 marks

(ii) Now both tuning forks are struck simultaneously and 10 beats are counted in a time of 5.000 s. Calculate the frequency produced by fork **B**.

2 marks

Question 21

Physics students use a sonometer (a stretched metal string) to conduct a series of experiments to study the production of sound using strings stretched over a sounding board. The device shown consists of a sounding board **A** (shaded), a fixed bridge support **B**, a moveable bridge support **C**, a frictionless pulley **D** and a weight **W** to control the string tension. An audio spectrum analyzer allows the measurement of frequency of the notes.

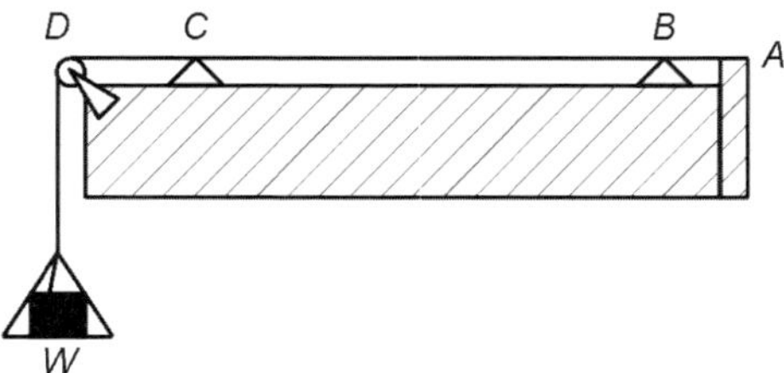

With the distance BC set at 1.08 m, a first harmonic is produced of frequency of 196.0 Hz.

(a) Calculate the speed of the wave in the string.

2 marks

The distance BC is now set at 0.75 m.

(b) Calculate the frequency of the first harmonic note now produced.

2 marks

The distance BC is restored to 1.08 m and the tension in the string increased by adding 10% more weight at **W**.

(c) What will happen to the frequency of the first harmonic note now produced – will it increase, stay the same or decrease? Give reasons.

2 marks

With distance BC still set at 1.08 m, the weight is restored back to **W** but the original string is replaced with one that has a greater linear density (kg m^{-1}).

(d) What will happen to the frequency of the first harmonic now produced – will it increase, stay the same or decrease? Give reasons.

2 marks

Question 22

It is sometimes possible to estimate the depth of a deep, dry well by clapping your hands together at the top of the well. You need the speed of sound to use this method. Describe what you would need to be able to hear after your clap to make this estimation, and the property of sound involved. Outline how you would calculate the depth of the well.

3 marks

Question 23

A hiker stands in front of a large cliff and lets off a cracker. The echo of the noise of the cracker reaches her 2.9 seconds later. The cliff is a distance of 500 m from the hiker. Use this information to calculate the speed of sound at the time.

3 marks

Question 24

A sketch of an outdoor amphitheatre is shown below. The 'steps' are made of stone, and reflect sound waves well. A tourist is standing facing the steps, as shown in the diagram.

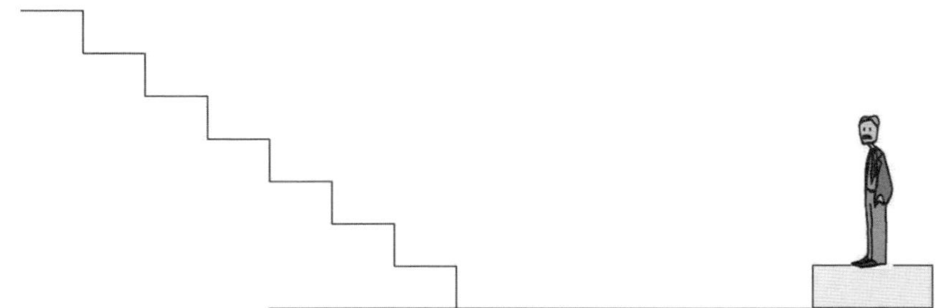

Describe carefully the echoes he will hear after he claps his hands together.

3 marks

Chapter 9 – Ray model of light

Question 1
Which *one or more* of the following is/are the best description(s) of the *image* formed by a convex mirror?

A. It can be magnified and virtual.
B. It is always virtual and diminished.
C. It can be diminished and real.
D. It can be magnified and real.

1 mark

Question 2
Which *one or more* of the following is/are the best description(s) of the *image* formed by a concave mirror?

A. It can be magnified and virtual.
B. It is always virtual and diminished.
C. It can be diminished and real.
D. It can be magnified and real.

1 mark

Question 3
Which *one or more* of the following is/are the best description(s) of the *image* formed by a concave lens?

A. It can be magnified and virtual.
B. It is always virtual and diminished.
C. It can be diminished and real.
D. It can be magnified and real.

1 mark

Question 4
Which *one or more* of the following is/are the best description(s) of the *image* formed by a convex lens?

A. It can be magnified and virtual.
B. It is always virtual and diminished.
C. It can be diminished and real.
D. It can be magnified and real.

1 mark

Question 5
Which of the following is the best description of a *security mirror* in a shop?

A. It is a convex mirror.
B. It is a plane mirror.
C. It is a concave mirror.
D. It can be all of the above.

1 mark

Question 6
Which of the following is the best description of the *reflecting mirror* in a Newtonian reflecting telescope?

A. It is a convex mirror.
B. It is a plane mirror.
C. It is a concave mirror.
D. It can be all of the above.

1 mark

Question 7

Which of the following is the best description of the *refractive index* of a material?

A. The ratio of the speed of light in a vacuum to the speed of light in the material.
B. The ratio of the speed of light in the material to the speed of light in a vacuum.
C. The ratio of the speed of light in the material to the speed of light in a reference material.
D. The ratio of the speed of light before reflection to the speed of light after reflection.

1 mark

Question 8

Which *one or more* of the following statements about reflection from a plane surface describes the relationship between incident (I), normal (N) and reflected (R) rays?

A. The angle between I and R is double the angle between I and N.
B. The angle between R and N is equal to the angle between I and R.
C. The angle between I and N is equal to the angle between R and N.
D. The plane created by I and N is the same as the plane created by R and N.

1 mark

Question 9

Which *one or more* of the following statements about internal reflection and the critical angle are correct statements?

A. Total internal reflection occurs when the incident angle is greater than the critical angle.
B. Total internal reflection occurs when the incident angle is less than the critical angle.
C. Partial internal reflection occurs when the incident angle is greater than the critical angle.
D. Partial internal reflection occurs when the incident angle is less than the critical angle.

1 mark

Question 10

An object is placed a distance $s = 2f$ from a *convex* mirror with focal length f and centre of curvature C as shown.

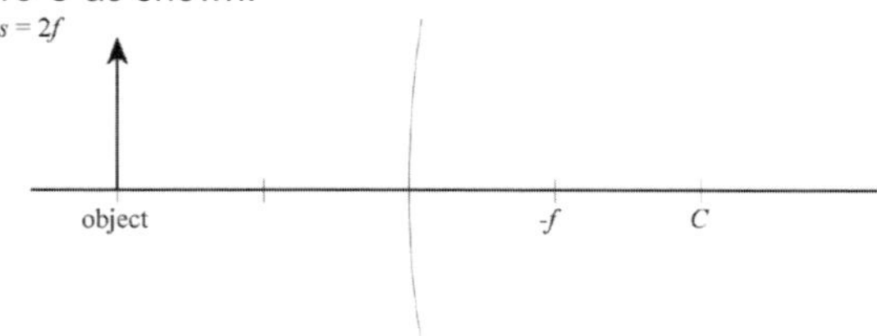

(a) Draw a diagram with 3 principal rays to find the location and size of the image.

3 marks

(b) Use the following to describe the nature of the image: real (R) or virtual (V); upright (U) or inverted (I); magnified (M), same size (SS) or diminished (D).

3 marks

Question 11

An object is placed a distance $s = 2f$ from a convex lens with focal length f as shown.

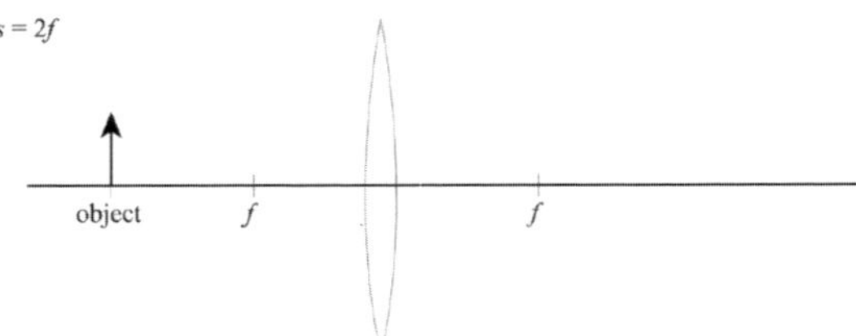

(a) Draw a diagram with 3 principal rays to find the location and size of the image.

3 marks

(b) Use the following to describe the nature of the image: real (R) or virtual (V); upright (U) or inverted (I); magnified (M), same size (SS) or diminished (D).

3 marks

Question 12

An object is placed a distance $s = 3f$ from a concave mirror with focal length f and centre of curvature C as shown.

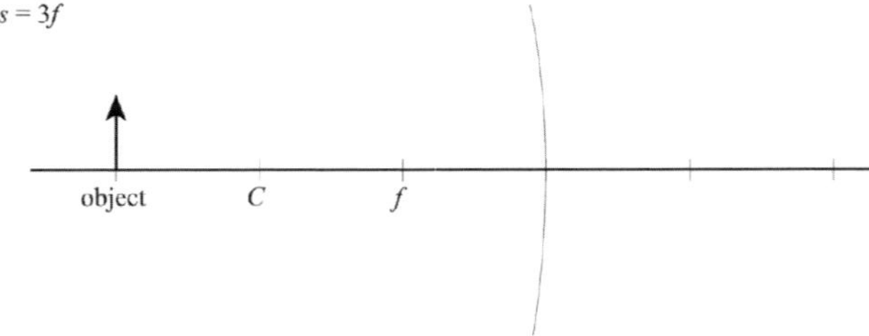

(a) Draw a ray diagram using 3 principal rays to find the location and size of the image.

3 marks

(b) Using the following to specify the nature of the image: real (R) or virtual (V); upright (U) or inverted (I); magnified (M), same size (SS) or diminished (D).

3 marks

Question 13

An object is placed a distance $s = 3f$ from a concave lens with focal length f as shown.

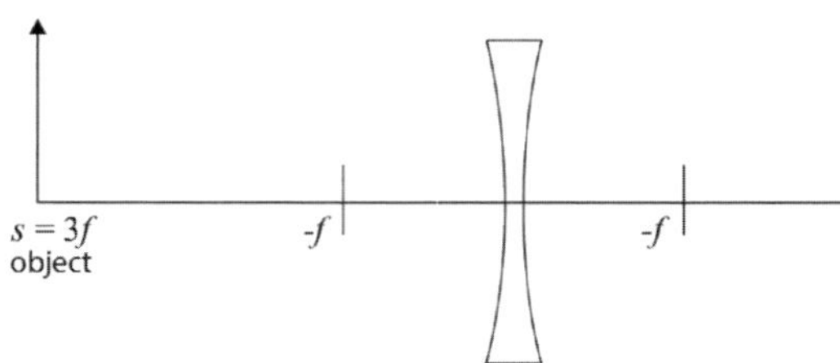

(a) Draw a ray diagram using 3 principal rays to find the location and size of the image.

3 marks

(b) Using the following to specify the nature of the image: real (R) or virtual (V); upright (U) or inverted (I); magnified (M), same size (SS) or diminished (D).

3 marks

Question 14

Light from a star in deep space spreads out equally in all directions. Scientists aboard the *Enterprise* measure the intensity of light from the star when they are 5.0 light-hours distant from the centre of the star to be 1.6 W m^{-2}. Calculate the intensity that they would measure if they were at a distance of 10 light-hours from the centre of the star.

3 marks

Question 15

A ray of blue light is incident on the triangular block of transparent material in the diagram. The angle *a* is equal to 50°. The transparent material is surrounded by air (n = 1.00).

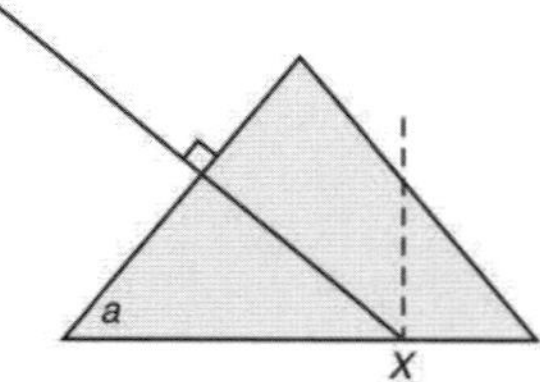

Calculate the minimum refractive index of the glass if the ray of light is to be totally internally reflected at the point *X*.

3 marks

Question 16

The refractive index of cubic zirconia is close to 2.15. Use this data to calculate the speed of light in cubic zirconia. Use $c = 3.00 \times 10^8$ m s^{-1}.

2 marks

Question 17

Cerenkov radiation occurs when particles of matter travel faster than the speed of light. This is only possible in materials with a refractive index greater than 1, because matter cannot travel faster than the speed of light in a vacuum (3.00×10^8 m s^{-1}). Calculate the speed of a particle in a crystal of diamond (n = 2.42) if it is to emit Cerenkov radiation.

3 marks

Question 18

Three different lasers (a red laser (R), a green laser (G) and a blue laser (B)) are used to shine light through a glass prism. Each laser beam has the same angle of incidence on the glass face.

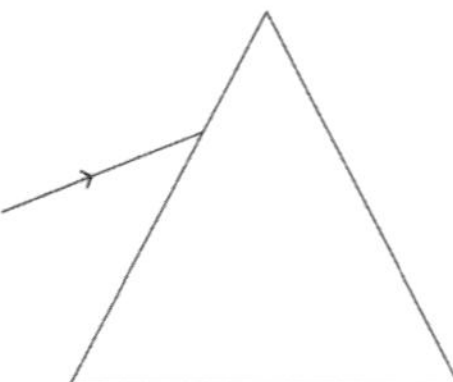

(a) Sketch the path of the light through the prism and out the other side for each of the three different coloured laser beams.

3 marks

(b) What is this phenomenon called?

1 mark

(c) Explain how this phenomenon occurs with reference to the refractive index of the glass.

3 marks

(d) Briefly outline how this phenomenon is related to the formation of rainbows.

2 marks

Question 19

Students perform an experiment sending rays of light from air (n = 1.00) into a rectangular plastic block.

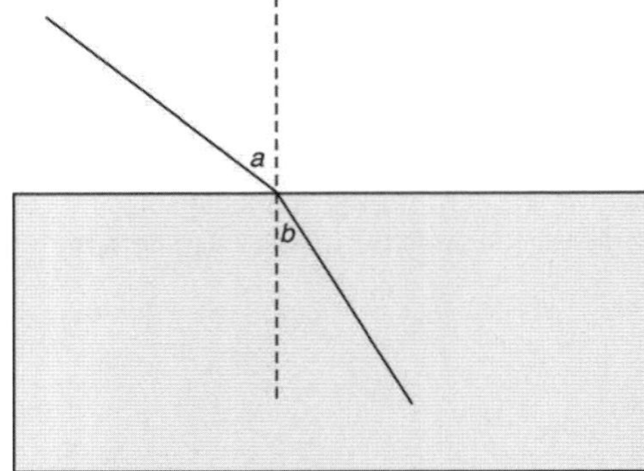

They measure the pairs of angles a and b for six different situations and plot the graph shown below.

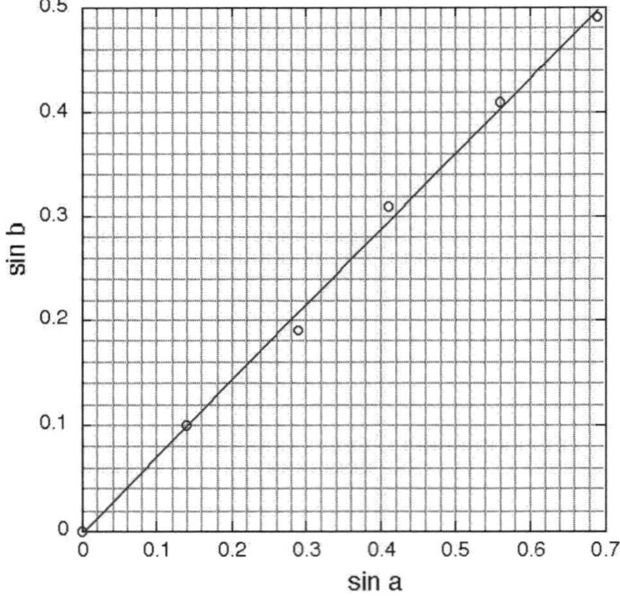

Use the graph to calculate the refractive index of the plastic. Show all the steps of your calculation.

4 marks

Question 20

A ray of light of wavelength 450 nm in air (n_{AIR} = 1.00) enters a block of plastic with n = 1.20. Take the speed of light in air to be 3.00×10^{8} m s^{-1}. Calculate:

(a) the speed of the light in the plastic
(b) the frequency of the light in air
(c) the frequency of the light in the plastic
(d) the wavelength of the light in the plastic

4 marks

Question 21

A light at the bottom of a fish tank sends two beams upwards to the surface as shown. (Take $n_{AIR} = 1.00$; $n_{WATER} = 1.33$)

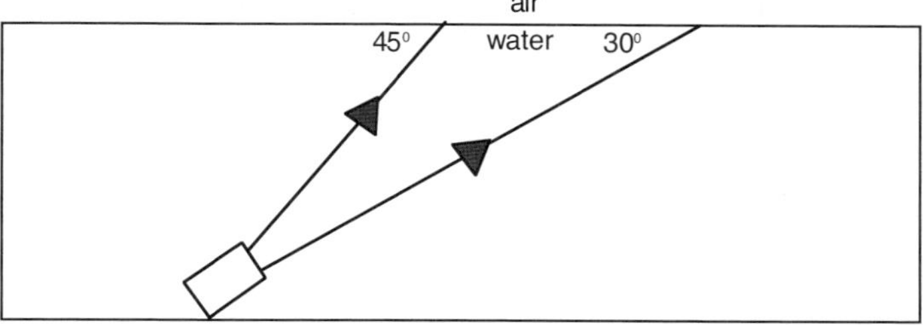

Use Snell's Law to calculate the path of the rays after they strike the water-air interface. Draw the ray paths you calculate on the diagram, marking any relevant angles carefully. Clarify all the steps of your calculations.

6 marks

Question 22

A fisherman looking at fish at night is trying to illuminate a particular fish by using a torch. The torch gives out a narrow beam of light. The diagram below shows the position of the torch, the water surface and the fish.

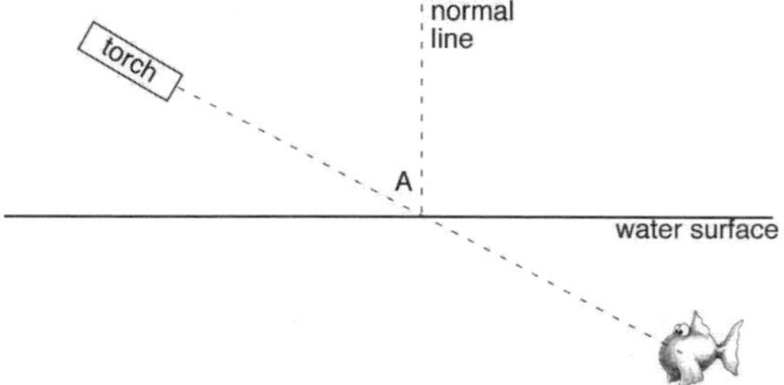

He finds that if he shines the torch directly at the fish (as shown in the diagram) the fish is *not* illuminated. Draw on the diagram the *approximate* position that he should direct the beam of light if the fish is to be illuminated, and explain your reasoning.

4 marks

Question 23

A student conducts an experiment with a small light source at the bottom of a tank of water.

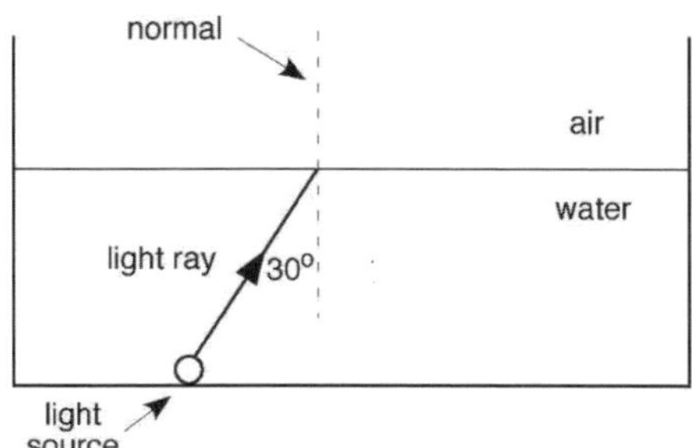

(a) Sketch on the diagram the path of the ray when it emerges from the water. Calculate the angle between the normal and the ray when the ray is in the air. Label this value on the diagram.

DATA: $n_{air} = 1.0$; $n_{water} = 1.3$

3 marks

(b) When the angle between the normal and the ray in water is increased beyond a certain *critical* value, the light ray does not emerge from the water. Calculate this critical angle in degrees.

2 marks

Question 24

The critical angle for an *underwater* optical fibre material is found to be 64°. If the refractive index of water is 1.33, calculate the refractive index of the test material. (there is no cladding on the optical fibre.)

2 marks

Question 25

A ray of yellow light (AB) of a single frequency falls on a rectangular glass block, as shown in the diagram below. The glass has a refractive index of 1.57; the air surrounding the glass block has n = 1.00. All the rays of light shown are of the same *frequency* as the ray AB. Some of them are fainter than others.

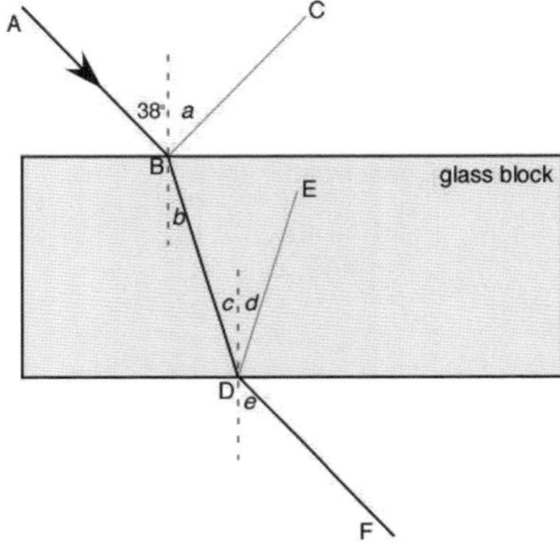

(a) Calculate the value of the angle b. Give your answer to two significant figures.

2 marks

(b) Calculate the values of the angles a, c, d, and e.

3 marks

(c) The ray DE continues past the point E. On the diagram above, carefully sketch the path of the light to the point where it meets the surface of the glass block, and for about 2 cm after that point.

2 marks

(d) The yellow ray of light is replaced by a single frequency ray of blue light. The blue light has a higher refractive index than the yellow light. Which of the following best describes how this affects the angles a, b and e in the diagram?

A. Angles a, b and e are all unchanged.
B. Angles a and e are unchanged, but angle b increases.
C. Angles a, b and e all increase.
D. Angles a and e are unchanged, but angle b decreases.

3 marks

Question 26

A *critical angle* can occur when light travels from a medium of higher refractive index to one of lower refractive index. Which one of the cases below has the *smallest* critical angle value?

A. Light travelling from glass (n = 1.50) to air (n = 1.00).

B. Light travelling from diamond (n = 2.42) to carbon tetrachloride (n = 1.63).
C. Light travelling from cubic zirconia (n = 2.18) to water (n = 1.33).
D. Light travelling from sphalerite (n = 2.37) to ethanol (n = 1.36).

3 marks

Question 27

The diagram below shows light rays travelling through a simple optical fibre.

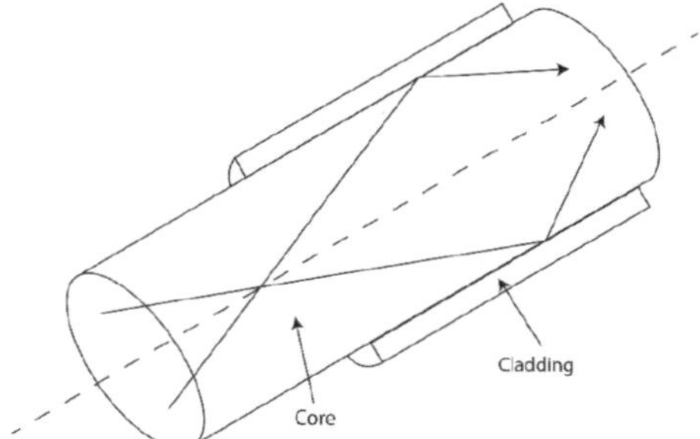

Analyse:

(a) the relative refractive indices of the core and the cladding.

2 marks

(b) how an optical fibre can still transmit the rays of light without loss when there is a bend in the fibre.

2 marks

Question 28

Laser light travelling underwater enters a diamond on the floor of the ocean. Diamond has a refractive index of 2.4; seawater has a refractive index of 1.3. Calculate the following ratios:

(a) speed of light in diamond/speed of light in seawater
(b) frequency of light in diamond/frequency of light in seawater
(c) wavelength of light in diamond/wavelength of light in seawater

3 marks

Question 29

The intensity of radiation from the Sun is 9.126 kW m^{-2} at the distance of Mercury (0.387 AU from the Sun's centre). Calculate the intensity of radiation from the Sun at Earth's surface (1.000 AU from the Sun's centre). 1 Astronomical Unit (AU) is approximately 150×10^6 km).

3 marks

Question 30

A famous story by H.G. Wells *The Invisible Man* describes a person who has made himself invisible to others by changing the refractive index of his body to that of air. Discuss the implications of this (if it were possible) to his ability to eat, his ability to see and his ability to keep warm on cold days.

3 marks

Chapter 10 – Thermodynamics

Question 1

(a) Which of the following is closest to 13°C?

A. 260 K
B. 273 K
C. 286 K
D. 296 K

1 mark

(b) Which of the following is closest to 303 K?

A. 30°C
B. 70°C
C. 130°C
D. 573°C

1 mark

Question 2

Which *one or more* of the following statements is correct?

A. When a block of aluminium at 300 K is in contact with a block of copper at 300 K, thermal energy will transfer into the block with the highest heat capacity.
B. When a block of aluminium at 300 K is in contact with a block of copper at 300 K, no thermal energy will transfer into or out of either block.
C. When a block of aluminium at 300 K is in contact with a block of copper at 300 K, the amount of thermal energy that transfers will depend on the relative conductivities of the two blocks.
D. When a block of aluminium at 300 K is in contact with a block of copper at 300 K, thermal energy will transfer out of the block with the highest heat capacity.

1 mark

Question 3

Label the following statements *True* or *False.*

(a) The temperature of a body is a measure of its heat capacity.
(b) The temperature of a body is a measure of the average KE of its molecules.
(c) When you use a thermometer accurately to measure someone's temperature, the person and the thermometer are in thermal equilibrium.
(d) The temperature of a body depends on its ability to conduct heat.
(e) Negative kelvin temperatures do not exist.
(f) There is an absolute minimum of temperature and also an absolute maximum of temperature.
(g) When an iron block at 75°C is immersed in water at 20°C, the thermal energy of the iron can increase and that of the water can decrease.
(h) If Body A is hotter than Body B, then it must have greater total thermal energy.

8 marks

Question 4

A cup of coffee, originally at 80°C, sits on a bench in a room that is at 20°C. Which of the following most accurately describes what happens?

A. The temperature of the coffee will cool to slightly below room temperature.
B. The temperature of the coffee will cool to exactly room temperature.
C. The final temperature of the coffee depends on how well insulated the cup is.
D. The temperature of the coffee will cool to slightly above room temperature.

1 mark

Question 5

Which of the following is closest to the thermal energy required to heat the water in a swimming pool of length 10 m, width 5.0 m and depth 2.0 m, from 10°C to 22°C? Neglect energy losses. Take the density of water as 1.0×10^3 kg m^{-3}.

A. 5.0×10^6 J

B. 4.2×10^8 J

C. 5.0×10^8 J

D. 5.0×10^9 J

1 mark

Question 6

A student plans to cool a room by placing a tank of very cold water in the middle of the room. The water is at 4°C, and the room is warmer. He wants to absorb 150 MJ of thermal energy until the water is at 22°C. Which of the following is closest to the number of kilograms of water he will need?

A. 200 kg

B. 2.00×10^3 kg

C. 2.00×10^4 kg

D. 2.00×10^6 kg

1 mark

Question 7

A square sheet of 4 mm thick glass in a window has an area of 0.64 m^2. A temperature difference of 12° across it allows thermal energy to pass through it at 2000 J s^{-1}. Which of the following is closest to the thermal conductivity of the glass?

A. 0.10 W m^{-1} K^{-1}

B. 1.0 W m^{-1} K^{-1}

C. 0.010 kW m^{-1} K^{-1}

D. 1.0 kW m^{-1} K^{-1}

1 mark

Question 8

Which of the following is the best description of the *thermal conductivity* of an insulating material with a temperature difference of 1 K across it?

A. The rate at which the temperature falls across 1 m of 1 m^2 of the material.

B. The rate at which energy passes though 1 m^2 of a 1 m thick piece of the material.

C. The thickness of 1 m^2 of the material required to reduce energy losses to zero.

D. The rate at which energy passes through a 1 m^2 piece of the material.

1 mark

Question 9

An architect has to choose between two glass windows. One, window A, has an area 0.50 m^2, glass of thickness 3.0 mm with a thermal conductivity 0.90. The other has an area of 0.30 m^2, thickness 2.0 mm and thermal conductivity 1.2. Which of the following is closest to the ratio of:

$$\frac{\text{Thermal energy loss rate through window B}}{\text{Thermal energy loss rate through window A}}?$$

A. 0.53

B. 0.83

C. 1.2

D. 1.3

1 mark

Question 10

One end of a uniform pipe is kept at a high temperature in a furnace while the other end is at 20°C. The rate at which thermal energy is transferred along the pipe depends on which *one or more* of the following?

A. The temperature difference between the two ends of the pipe
B. The length of the pipe
C. The thickness of the pipe
D. The kind of metal of the pipe

1 mark

Question 11

Explain what is meant by the concept of *thermal equilibrium.*

2 marks

Question 12

A 1.5 kg block of metal alloy is heated, raising its thermal energy by 4500 J. Its temperature rises by 5.0°C. Calculate the specific heat capacity of the alloy.

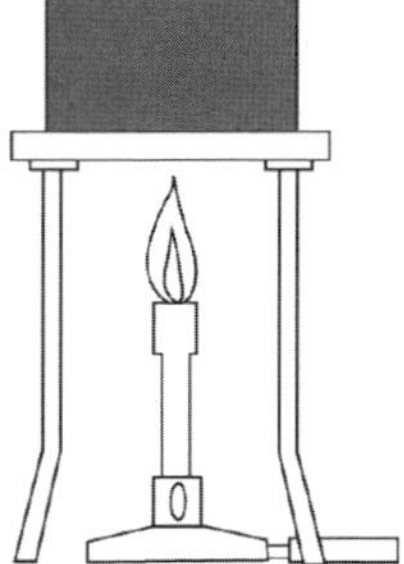

2 marks

Question 13

Calculate the total thermal energy required to change 2.0 kg of water at 20°C to steam at 100°C. Take the latent heat of vaporisation of water as 2.26 MJ kg^{-1}.

4 marks

Question 14

A 15 g block of ice at 273 K is added to 100 g of water at 333 K. The ice all melts, and the resulting water is at a cooler temperature. Calculate this temperature. You can assume that there is no transfer of thermal energy to the environment.

4 marks

Question 15

Explain why a kilogram of steam at 373 K will probably cause more severe burns than a kilogram of water at the same temperature.

3 marks

Question 16

At many seaside locations, the temperature variations during the summer are generally less, and it is cooler than at inland locations. Discuss thermodynamic factors related to this.

3 marks

Question 17

Calculate the total cost of converting 2.0 kg of ice (at 0°C) to steam, if the cost of energy is 3.1 c MJ^{-1}.

4 marks

Question 18

When a volatile liquid (for example, methylated spirits) spills on you hand, it feels cold. Discuss.

3 marks

Question 19

(a) On a hot day, some houses warm more slowly than others. These are sometimes referred to as having a high 'thermal mass'. Outline factors that would contribute to a high thermal mass.

3 marks

(b) Discuss whether high thermal mass houses would be more or less difficult to heat up in cold weather.

3 marks

Question 20

When soups contain a large proportion of solid material (e.g. vegetables) compared to water, they tend to cool more quickly. Discuss.

3 marks

Question 21

A student thoroughly mixes some crushed ice with some cold water in an insulated container. After some time, the ice does not melt further and the water does not freeze. What is the temperature of the mixture in K?

1 mark

Question 22

A student heats a sample of ice from less than 0°C to a temperature above 100°C. She measures the temperature as a function of time and graphs the results. An idealised version of the graph is shown below. Discuss the shape of the graph, including the transitions between different gradients.

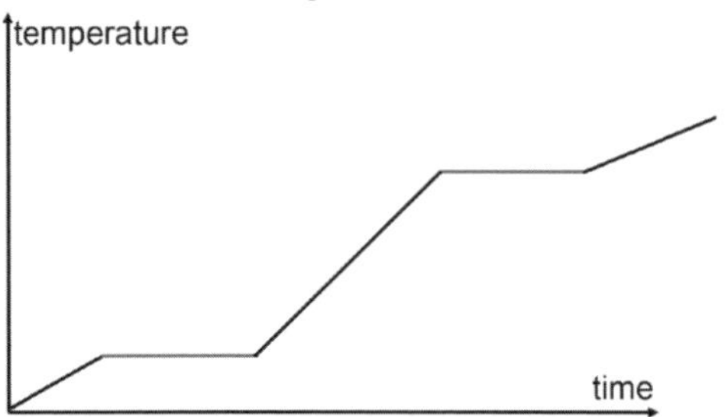

4 marks

Question 23

On windy days, wet washing hanging on a clothesline is generally colder than on a still day, even if the amount of sunlight and the air temperature is the same. Discuss.

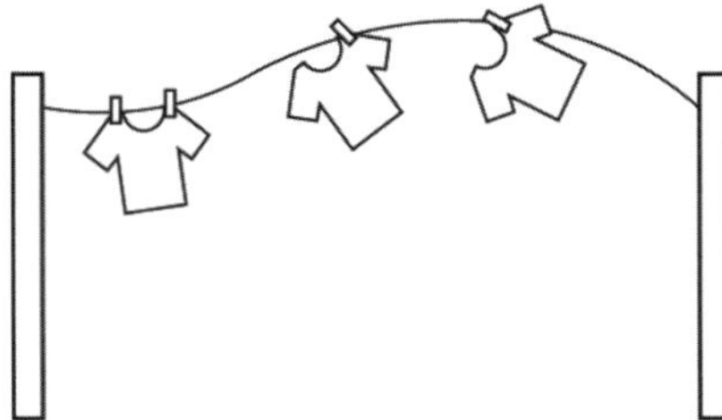

3 marks

Question 24

Discuss how sweating helps you to cool down.

3 marks

Question 25

(a) An 'adventure sports' website advises outdoor adventurers to 'beware of wet and wind' in order to avoid the condition of *hypothermia* (the dangerous lowering of body temperature). Discuss.

3 marks

(b) Other websites dealing with *hyperthermia* (the dangerous raising of body temperature) advise fanning and water on the skin of victims. Discuss.

3 marks

Question 26

Some builders of 'energy efficient' houses advocate including interior walls whose cavities are filled with water (rather than air or wood or stone). Discuss.

3 marks

Question 27

A room is warmed up using a heat pump that provides a constant amount of thermal energy to the room. Initially the room is cold (10°C) and the temperature rises rapidly, but as it warms up, the rate of temperature change decreases, and eventually slows to zero, although the heat pump is operating correctly. Discuss why the rate of temperature rise slows as the temperature of the room increases, and eventually reaches zero.

3 marks

Question 28

Scientists are testing heaters to calculate their effectiveness, in terms of the thermal energy they provide every second. They build a six-sided cube; each side has an area of 1.0 m^2 and a thickness of 30 mm. The thermal conductivity of the walls is equal to 5.0 W m^{-1} K^{-1}.

(a) In the first trial, the temperature increases until there is a difference of 15°C between the inside and the outside of the box, and does not increase further. Calculate the power of the heater.

3 marks

(b) In the second trial, the power of the heater is increased by 30%. What is the temperature difference when equilibrium is now reached?

2 marks

Question 29

A cup of freshly brewed coffee sits on a table. Describe the various ways in which thermal energy transfers from the hot coffee to the cooler environment.

3 marks

Question 30

A silver spoon is placed in a hot cup of tea. After a short time, the handle of the spoon becomes much warmer. Describe the mechanism by which thermal energy is transferred along the spoon.

3 marks

Question 31

Many modern houses, particularly in colder climates, make use of clear *double glazed windows* to reduce thermal energy losses through them. They are useful in reducing conduction losses through the windows.

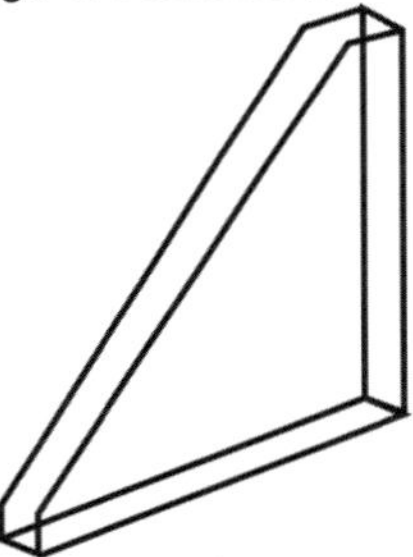

(a) Explain how these windows reduce conduction losses (remember that glass is a poor insulator).

2 marks

(b) The gap is sometimes filled with argon gas or a vacuum. Discuss briefly the possible reason for these options.

2 marks

(c) If a gas is used between the glass sheets, the gap width should not be too large (for best performance). Discuss.

2 marks

Question 32

On cold days, many people wear clothing that contains pockets of small feathers (puffer jackets). The small feathers are sometimes called *down.* Outline two thermal energy transfer mechanisms that these pockets of feathers reduce.

3 marks

Question 33

Kitchen cooking appliances use various methods of thermal energy transfer. Identify the main method(s) used in each of the following examples.

(a) Reheating leftovers in a microwave oven
(b) Cooking toast
(c) Frying eggs
(d) Cooking a cake in an electric oven with the fan operating
(e) Boiling water in an electric kettle

5 marks

Question 34
Suggest why people sometimes prefer mittens to gloves in cold weather.

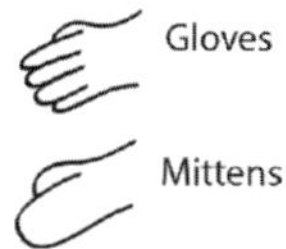

2 marks

Question 35
Saucepans are sometimes manufactured with a copper layer on their bottom surface. Suggest a reason for this construction.

2 marks

Question 36
The pattern of air movement in a room with a wall heater can look like that shown in the diagram below.

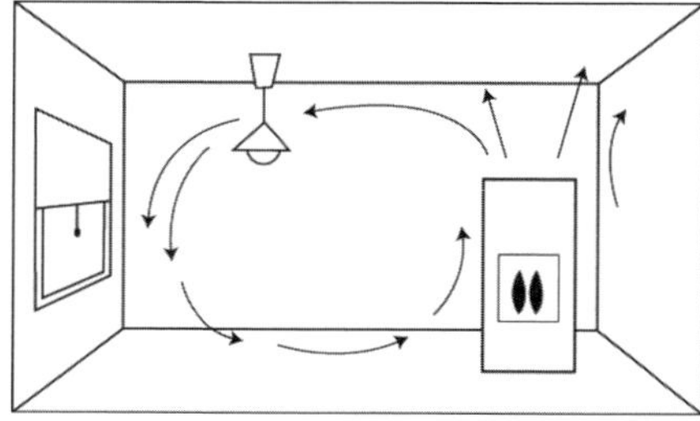

This is called 'natural' convection. Discuss why it occurs.

3 marks

Question 37
Ceiling fans are often only associated with cooling during the summer, but if run slowly in winter they can help warm the whole room. Discuss why.

3 marks

Question 38
Describe how convection is involved in creating 'sea breezes' near the coast.

2 marks

Question 39
Many modern ovens are fitted with a fan to circulate the air. Suggest when it could be useful to turn the fan on, and when it could be useful to leave the fan off.

2 marks

Question 40
A vacuum flask can be used to keep drinks hot or cold (for example). Explain how they reduce heat transfer by convection, conduction, radiation and evaporation.

3 marks

Question 41
Briefly summarise why the inside of a car warms up on a cold but sunny day.

3 marks

Chapter 11 – Electrostatics

Question 1

A plastic ruler when rubbed on your jeans becomes negatively charged. What is the net charge on the part of your jeans that you rubbed?

A. Negative
B. Zero
C. Positive
D. Cannot be determined from the information given

1 mark

Question 2

A small positively charged rod is brought near to two isolated conducting spheres A and B as shown.

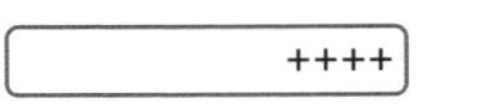

(a) What is the net charge on spheres A and B?

A. Negative
B. Zero
C. Positive
D. Cannot be determined from the information given

1 mark

(b) What is the net charge on sphere B?

A. Negative
B. Zero
C. Positive
D. Cannot be determined from the information given

1 mark

Question 3

Which one of the following statements is true concerning equipotential lines?

A. They are parallel to electric fields.
B. They are perpendicular to electric fields.
C. They are anti-parallel to electric fields.
D. None of the above.

1 mark

Question 4

Which one of the following best describes the work done on a positive charge travelling along an equipotential (a line of equal potential)?

A. Positive work is done by the field.
B. There is no work done by the field.
C. Negative work is done by the field.
D. It cannot be determined from the information given.

1 mark

Question 5

A girl walks on an acrylic carpet with insulating soles on her shoes and notices she gets a shock when she touches the metal doorknob. The effect is less on humid days. Explain.

4 marks

Question 6

A positively charged rod is held next to a small stream of water as shown below.

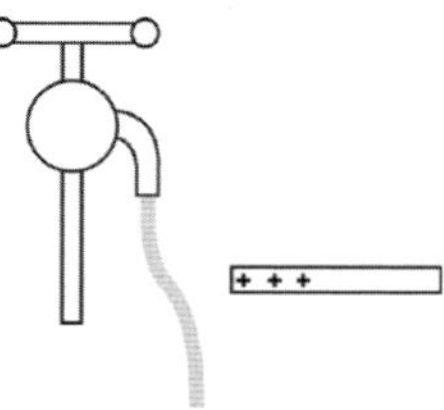

Explain why the water is deflected by the positively charged rod.

3 marks

Question 7

Positive charge is placed on the metal shape shown below. Draw the charge distribution on and the electric field around the charged metal shape.

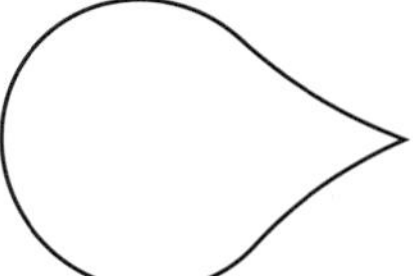

3 marks

Question 8

Sketch the electric fields between and around the charges in the two diagrams below.

(a)

2 marks

(b)

+2Q　　-Q

2 marks

Question 9

Two charged metal spheres of opposite sign are placed as shown below. The magnitude of the charges on the spheres is identical.

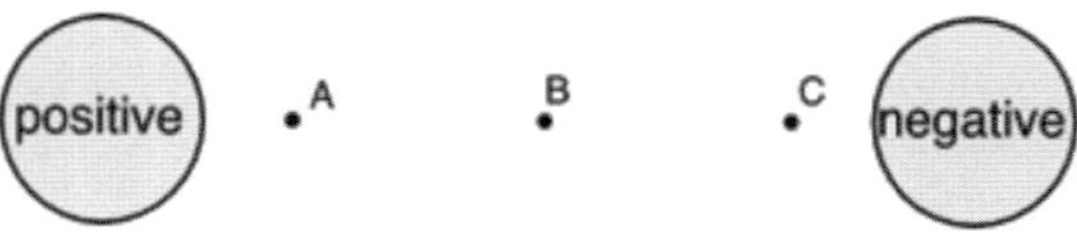

(a) Sketch the shape and direction of the electric field lines in the space between and around the charged spheres.

2 marks

(b) The points A, B and C lie on the line joining the sphere centres. B is equidistant from both spheres, and A and C are the same distance from the sphere they are each closest to. Estimate the relative strength and direction of the electric field at points A, B and C.

2 marks

(c) Describe the electric field at B if both large spheres carry charge of the *same* sign.

2 marks

Question 10

Two positive charges (Q_1 and Q_2) are placed on insulated metal spheres a distance of 10 cm apart as shown.

DATA: $Q_1 = +8.0 \times 10^{-10}$ C and $Q_2 = 5.0 \times 10^{-10}$ C.

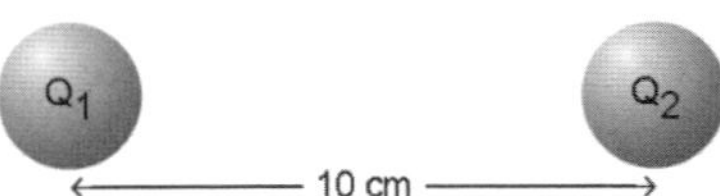

(a) Calculate the magnitude of the electric force acting on the spheres.

2 marks

(b) Describe the direction of the electric force between the two spheres. Give reasons for your answer.

2 marks

(c) Determine the magnitude of the electric force between the two spheres if the distance is decreased from 10 cm to 5 cm.

2 marks

Question 11

Three insulated conducting spheres P, Q and R all have equal charges on them. They are placed as shown. Sphere P exerts a force of 4.0×10^{-6} N on sphere R.

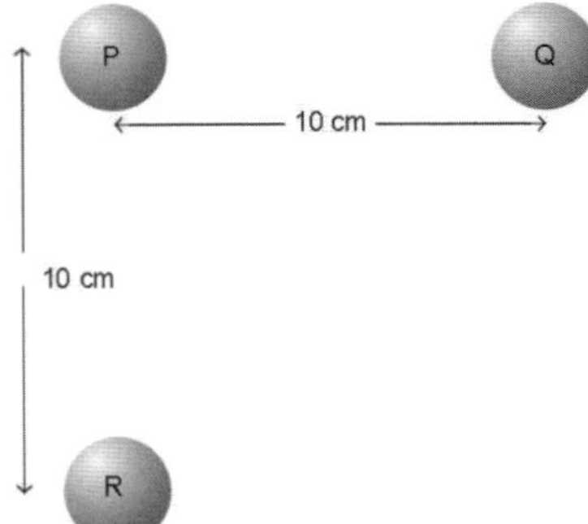

(a) Calculate the magnitude of the force that sphere P exerts on sphere Q.

2 marks

(b) Calculate the magnitude and direction of the net force on sphere P.

3 marks

Question 12

The diagram below shows the two parallel plates of a capacitor connected to a battery. The space between the plates is evacuated of air.

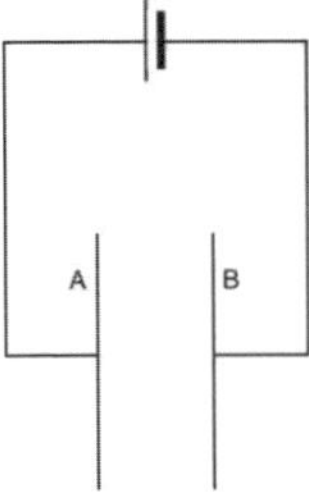

(a) Sketch the electric field lines in the space between the plates. Include the direction of the field.

2 marks

(b) Sketch 2 equipotential lines between the capacitor plates.

2 marks

(c) An electron is introduced into the space between the plates. It experiences an electric force of magnitude 3.20×10^{-14} N. Calculate the magnitude and direction of the electric field between the plates.

3 marks

(d) An alpha-particle (charge = $+3.20 \times 10^{-19}$ C) is now introduced into the space between the plates. Compare the electric force that the alpha particle experiences with the force that the electron experiences.

2 marks

(e) A small charged particle of unknown charge q is now introduced between the plates. It experiences a force towards plate B of magnitude 1.92×10^{-13} N. Calculate the magnitude and sign of q.

2 marks

Question 13

A uniform electric field exists between two charged plates as shown. The voltage between the plates is 20 V; the distance between the plates is 5.0 cm. An electron is placed on the bottom plate.

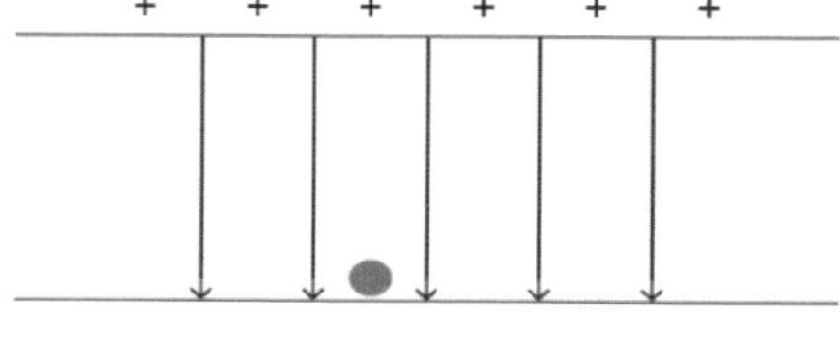

(a) Calculate the magnitude of the electric field between the two plates.

2 marks

(b) Calculate the magnitude of the electric force acting on the electron.

2 marks

(c) Calculate the work done on the electron as it moves from the bottom plate to the top plate.

2 marks

(d) Calculate the kinetic energy of the electron when it arrives at the top plate.

2 marks

The distance between the plates is doubled to 10.0 cm; voltage and charge are unchanged.

(e) Calculate the magnitude of the electric field between the two charged plates.

2 marks

(f) Calculate the magnitude of the electric force acting on the electron.

2 marks

(g) Calculate the kinetic energy the electron has when it arrives at the top plate.

2 marks

Chapter 12 – Electric circuits

Question 1

State the SI unit for the following quantities

(a) electric charge
(b) potential difference
(c) current
(d) power
(e) energy

5 marks

Question 2

Which one or more of the following statements correctly identifies a pair of equivalent units?

A. $N\ C^{-1}$ and $V\ m^{-1}$
B. $J\ C^{-1}$ and V
C. $V\ A^{-1}$ and Ω
D. $J\ s^{-1}$ and W

1 mark

Question 3

The flow of current in metals is due to

A. the movement of both positive and negative charges.
B. the movement of positive charges.
C. the movement of negative ions.
D. the movement of negative charges.

1 mark

Question 4

A device counting electrons that are moving in a metal wire measures 6.3×10^{18} electrons passing a point in a time of 10 seconds. The current due to this movement is closest to

A. 0.1 mA
B. 1 mA
C. 10 mA
D. 100 mA

1 mark

Question 5

Which one or more of the following affects the current flowing in a metal wire?

A. The size of the charge on electrons
B. The speed of the moving electrons
C. The number of electrons that are free to move in the metal
D. The density of the metal

1 mark

Question 6

A battery is firstly used to power to operate one clock and then two identical clocks connected in *parallel*. Which of the following is correct?

A. Connection in parallel reduces total resistance and increases battery life.
B. Connection in parallel increases total resistance and increases battery life.
C. Connection in parallel reduces total resistance and decreases battery life.
D. Connection in parallel increases total resistance and decreases battery life.

1 mark

Question 7

Which *one or more* of the following are possible units for energy?

A. watt (W)
B. volt-ampere (V A)
C. watt hour (W h)
D. volt-ampere-second (V A s)

1 mark

Question 8

A person accidentally touches a 240 V connection inside a toaster while it is operating. His resistance at the time is 20 kΩ. Which of the following is the closest to the current flowing through him as a result?

A. 1.0 mA
B. 10 mA
C. 0.10 A
D. 1.0 A

1 mark

Question 9

A battery is described as having a capacity of 100 ampere-hours. Which of the following does this rating most closely describe?

A. The maximum life to be expected from the battery.
B. The maximum energy capacity of the battery.
C. The maximum charge storage capacity of the battery.
D. The maximum current that can be expected from the battery.

1 mark

Question 10

The circuit for a small set of eight Christmas tree lights is shown below.

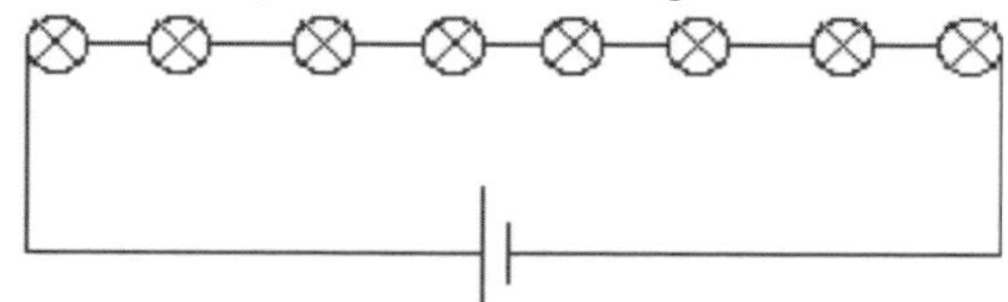

The voltage supply (shown above as a DC battery) is 240 V. The complete circuit is designed to consume a total of 160 W. Which of the following best describes the correct labelling for each light in the circuit?

A. 20 W; 30 V
B. 20 W; 240 V
C. 160 W; 30 V
D. 30 W; 20 V

1 mark

Question 11

A piece of conducting material can be shaped into different forms, without changing the volume. The material is originally a right circular cylinder of cross-section area 2.0 cm^2 and length 10 cm. It is reshaped into a right circular cylinder of length 40 cm and cross-section area 0.5 cm^2. Which one of the following best describes the effect of this on the average resistance of the piece of material?

A. The resistance will remain unchanged; the material is the same.
B. The resistance will increase by a factor greater than 10.
C. The resistance will increase by a factor of 4.
D. The resistance will decrease by a factor of 4.

1 mark

Question 12
Which *one or more* of the following are likely to *lower* the resistance of a conductor made of a particular metal?

A. Reduce the temperature of the conductor
B. Lengthen the conductor
C. Shorten the conductor
D. Decrease the cross-section area of the conductor

1 mark

Question 13
Tzin's small shack has the following appliances connected to a 250 V mains supply.

Appliance	*Resistance*
Main room light	500 Ω
Bedroom light	1000 Ω

Appliance	*Resistance*
Television	500 Ω
Refrigerator	250 Ω

Calculate the total resistance of these devices *all* connected in *parallel*.

3 marks

Question 14
An electric kettle has a working resistance of 6 ohm and a power output of 2.4 kW. Calculate its operating voltage.

2 marks

Question 15
Calculate the resistance of a 240 V electrical appliance rated at 2400 W.

2 marks

Question 16
Calculate the thermal energy, in MJ, produced by an efficient electric radiator in 24 hours when it is connected to a 100 V supply, and drawing a current of 5 A.

2 marks

Question 17
An electric motor uses 104 kW h of energy in a period of 48 hours, when connected to a 240 V voltage source. Calculate the average current flowing in the motor.

2 marks

Question 18
An electric heater of working resistance 4 ohm consumes 4.8×10^4 J over a period of 10 minutes.

(a) Calculate the size of the current drawn by the heater.

2 marks

(b) Calculate, in watts, the power input of the heater.

2 marks

Question 19
A power appliance is rated at 750 W when operating from 240 V. Calculate the power input when the appliance is connected to a 120 V voltage supply. Assume that the resistance of the appliance does not change.

2 marks

Question 20
All electrons carry the same amount of electric charge. Calculate the number of excess electrons required on an object for it to have a total charge of –10 C.

2 marks

Question 21
A battery in a motor vehicle draws 200 A when starting the car. This takes 3.0 s. Calculate how much charge the battery supplies to the starter motor during this time.

2 marks

Question 22
A household electricity bill states that, over 30 days, the average current was 25 A. Calculate the total charge supplied during that time.

2 marks

Question 23

During a lightning stroke, a charge of approximately 5.0 C is delivered. The average current during the stroke was 30 000 A. Calculate the time taken for the stroke.

2 marks

Question 24

Students conduct a first-hand investigation with a small torch globe. They connect the globe in series with a variable source of voltage and an ammeter. As they increase the voltage across the globe, the current increases. Describe how they would detect whether the resistance changes as the globes become brighter.

2 marks

Question 25

In a chemical experiment of a conducting liquid, investigation reveals that connecting a battery across the liquid causes the movement of electrons in one direction and positively charged ions in the opposite direction. The ions carry a charge of $+1.6 \times 10^{-19}$ C. The total current flowing is 500 mA. Calculate the number of ions passing any point in the liquid each second.

2 marks

Question 26

Students investigating the properties of a piece of conducting material connect it into the circuit shown below. The battery shown in the circuit has a continuously variable voltage output, from 0 to 12 V.

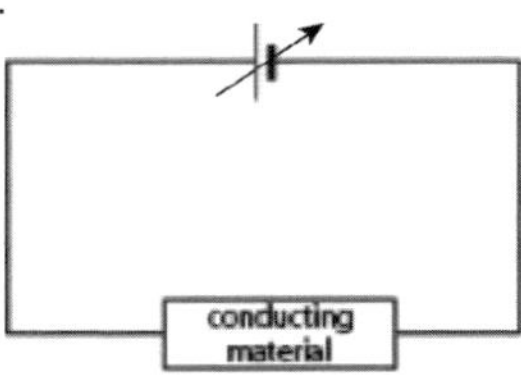

(a) The students wish to take a series of measurements of a range of different voltages across and currents through the conducting material. Redraw the circuit showing the correct placement of a voltmeter and an ammeter in the circuit.

3 marks

(b) The students measure a range of voltages and currents, as shown in the table.

Voltage (V)	0	2.0	4.9	8.3	10.1	12
Current (mA)	0	31	83	142	165	207

Graph these values on the grid below. Label the axes correctly, and draw a line of best fit through the points.

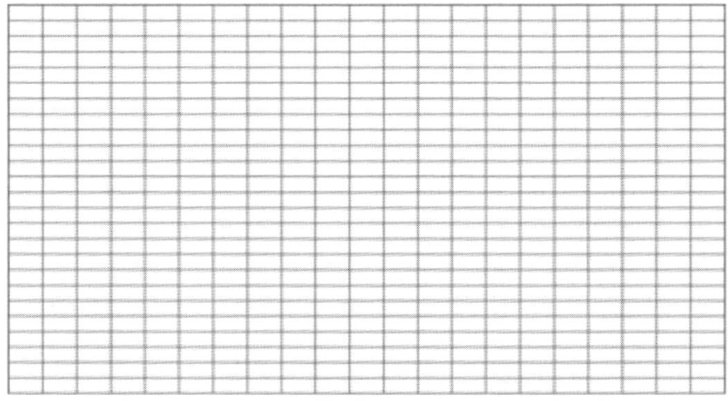

4 marks

(c) Use your graph to calculate the average resistance of the piece of material. Identify whether the material is ohmic or non-ohmic

4 marks

Question 27

The *I* - *V* graph of a light globe is shown in the graph below.

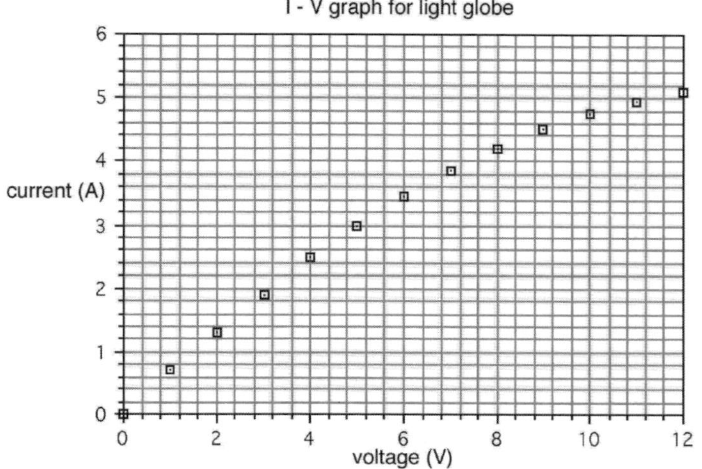

Calculate the ratio:

$$\frac{\text{resistance of light globe at 6 V}}{\text{resistance of light globe at 12 V}}$$

2 marks

Question 28

Summarise a key reason that enables most metals to be good conductors of electricity, but means that most plastics are poor conductors of electricity.

2 marks

Question 29

A DC circuit of one battery and a number of identical resistors is shown below. The potential difference across resistor 4 is 4.8 V. The battery supplies 12 V.

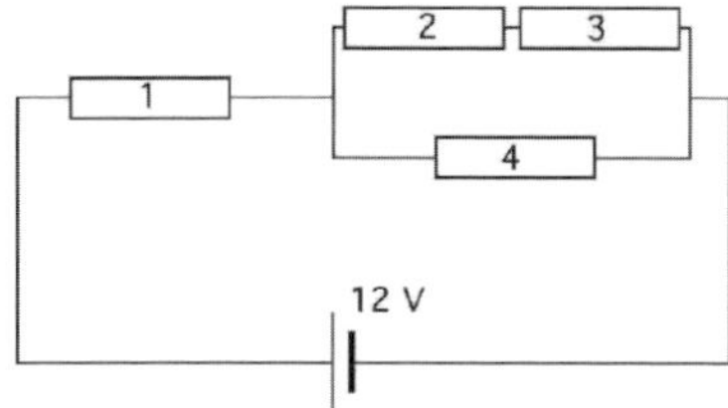

(a) Calculate how much potential energy is lost by one coulomb of charge flowing through resistor 4.

2 marks

(b) Calculate how much potential energy is lost by one coulomb of charge flowing through resistor 1.

2 marks

(c) Calculate how much potential energy is lost by one coulomb of charge flowing through resistor 2.

2 marks

(d) Calculate how much potential energy is gained by one coulomb of charge flowing through the battery.

2 marks

Question 30

The circuit diagram below shows two identical headlamps and two identical warning lamps. The warning lamps are fitted on to the dash of the car. They indicate that the headlamps are operating. The battery provides 12 V and a total current of 8.0 A.

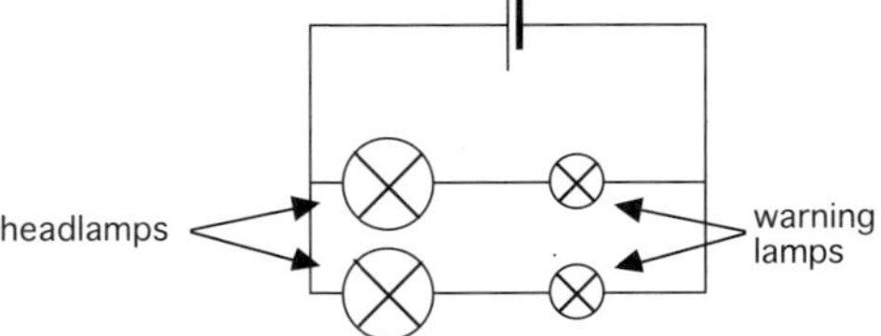

(a) Account for why the warning lights are wired in *series* with the headlamps.
2 marks

(b) Account for why the headlamps are connected in parallel.
2 marks

(c) Calculate the current through a warning light.
2 marks

(d) The voltage across a headlamp is 11.5 V. What is the voltage across a warning lamp?
2 marks

(e) Calculate the resistance of each warning light.
2 marks

Question 31

An electric blanket is made up of two resistors that carry current and heat up. The resistors can be connected in three ways, as shown in the diagrams below. Both resistors have exactly the same value of 120 ohms.

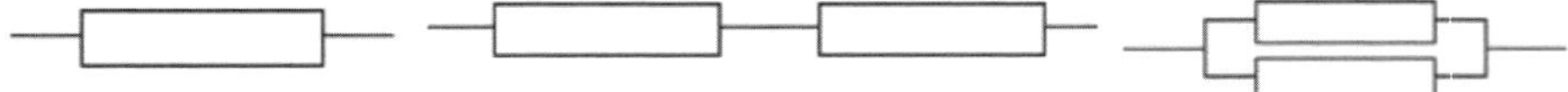

One resistor *Two resistors in series* *Two parallel resistors*

Calculate the current through each combination if each combination is connected to a voltage supply of 120 V.
3 marks

Question 32

In a normal domestic electrical system, all electrical appliances (including the lights) are connected in parallel, rather than in series. Identify *two* significant advantages of connecting them in this fashion.
2 marks

Question 33

In the circuit below, the fixed resistor has a value of 100 Ω, and the variable resistor can be adjusted between 0 and 200 Ω.

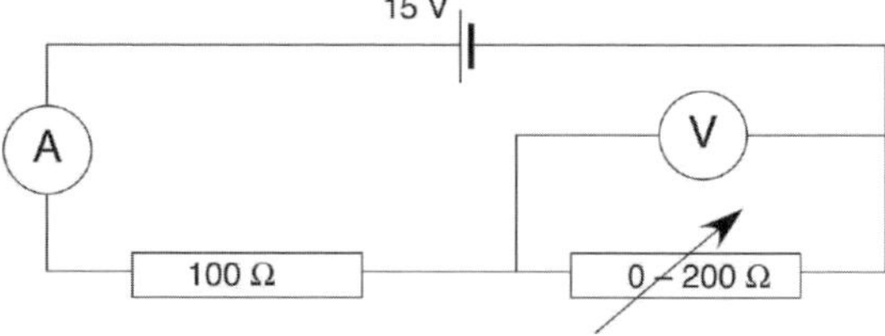

(a) Calculate the maximum and minimum values of the current possible through the ammeter.
2 marks

(b) Calculate the maximum and minimum voltage across the variable resistor.
2 marks

Question 34

Ammeters should have a very low resistance. Explain why.

2 marks

Question 35

Voltmeters should have a very high resistance. Explain why.

2 marks

Question 36

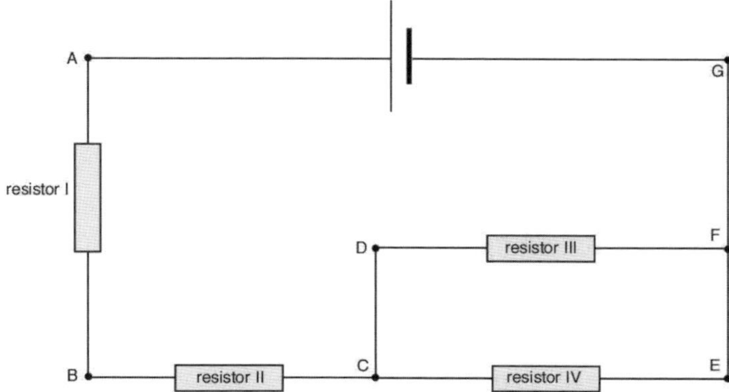

(a) Identify two resistors in series and two resistors in parallel in the circuit above.

2 marks

(b) All the resistors in the circuit have a value of 6.0 ohm. The battery has an output voltage of 15.0 V. The current through resistor III is 500 mA. Calculate

(i) the current through resistor I.
(ii) the current through resistor II.
(iii) the current through resistor IV.
(iv) the current through the battery.

4 marks

(c) Calculate the potential difference across the following pairs of points: AB, BC, CF, FG and AG.

5 marks

Question 37

Sarina is replacing the fuse wire in a fuse holder. Having nothing else to do, she decides to conduct a first-hand investigation of the piece of fuse wire. The circuit she uses is shown below.

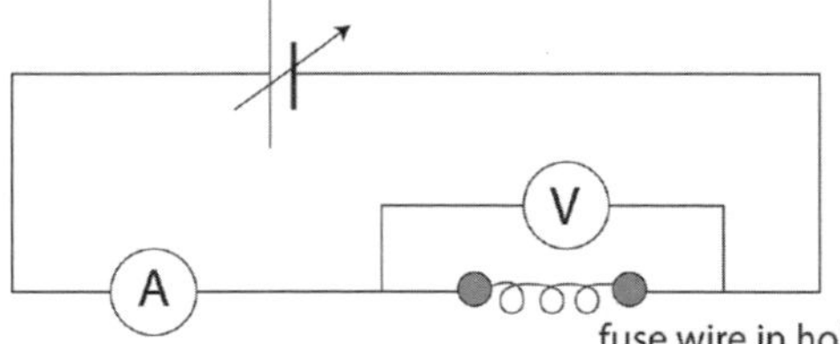

She varies the power supply voltage, and measures the values on the ammeter and the voltmeter. Her results are shown below. She keeps the piece of fuse wire constant throughout the experiment.

V (volts)	0	2	4	6	8	10	12
I (mA)	0	329	682	987	1350	1650	2030

(a) Graph the voltage against the current, and label the axes correctly. Put the current on the horizontal axis. Draw a line of best fit through the data points.

4 marks

(b) Use the graph to calculate the average resistance of the wire sample in the region between 0 and 12 volts. Show your reasoning.

3 marks

(c) Justify the description of the wire as 'ohmic'.

1 mark

(d) She now connects two identical samples of the fuse wire (of the same length as in the experiment on the previous page) in *series*. Calculate the resistance of this combination.

2 marks

(e) Calculate the total resistance if the two identical samples are in *parallel*.

2 marks

Question 38

Draw a circuit with the following components and arrangement.

- one 12 V battery
- three resistors of 6 ohm value each
- two resistors in parallel with each other (but not with the third resistor)
- the current through the battery equal to the current through one of the resistors

3 marks

Question 39

All the resistors in the diagram below have the same value, 5.0 ohms. The current through resistor D is measured to be 0.20 A.

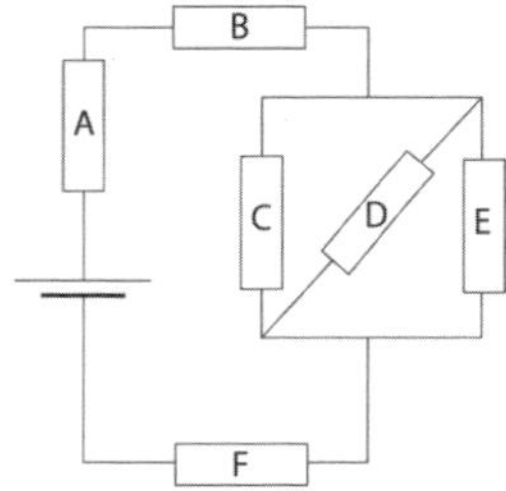

(a) Calculate the current through resistor E.

1 mark

(b) Calculate the current through resistor C.

1 mark

(c) Explain why the current through resistors A, B and F has the same value, and calculate that value.

3 marks

(d) Explain why the potential difference across resistors C, D and E has the same value, and calculate that value.

3 marks

(e) Use your answers to the previous questions (or otherwise) to calculate the voltage output of the battery. Show all the steps of your reasoning.

4 marks

Question 40

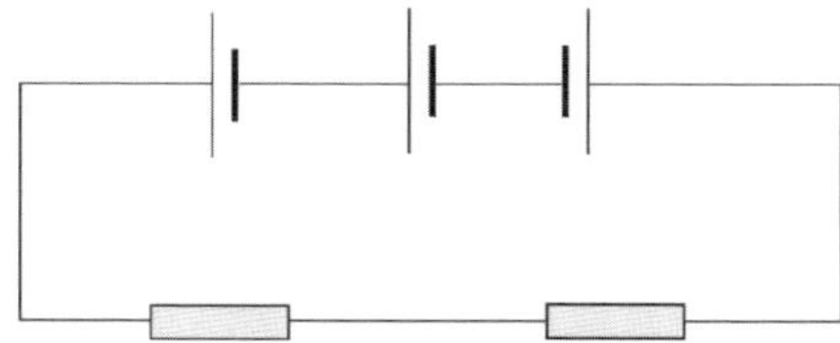

(a) The resistors are identical in the circuit above and the batteries each have a 6.0 V voltage. Calculate the potential difference across each of the resistors.

2 marks

(b) The current through one of the batteries is measured as 1.8 A. Calculate the value of each of the resistors. Show your working.

3 marks

Question 41

In the circuits below, some voltmeters and some ammeters are connected incorrectly. Identify these, and describe the effect this mistake would have.

(A)

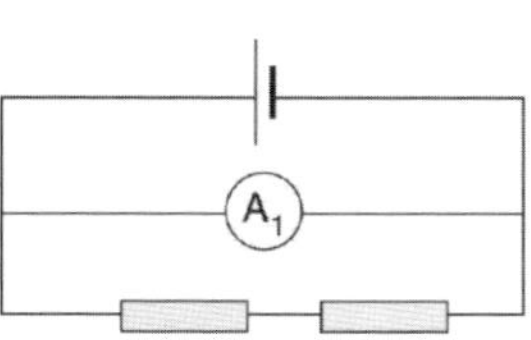

(B)

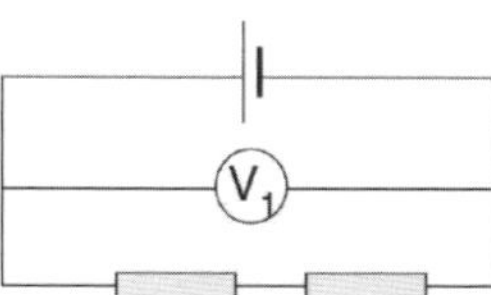

(C)

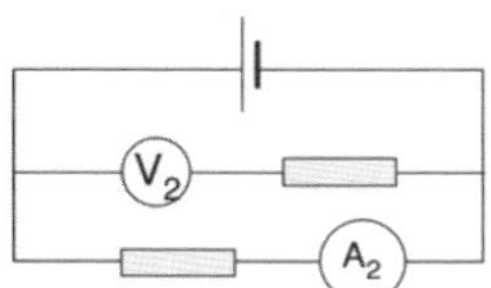

(D)

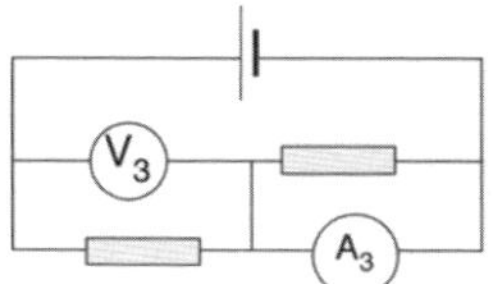

6 marks

Question 42

Household energy bills can be expressed in units of kilowatt-hour (kW h). One household uses 1.08×10^8 J of energy during a day. Calculate this in units of kW h.

3 marks

Question 43

A 12 V car battery is used in a remote house to power lighting and a radio. The circuit of the house is shown in the diagram below.

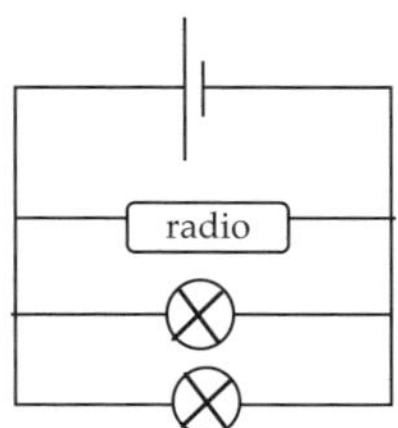

The lights both have a power rating of 60 W, and the radio has a power rating of 30 W, when running off a 12 V battery. Calculate the total current drain from the battery when the radio and both lights are switched on.

2 marks

Question 44

Arrange the following items into a circuit designed to give a total light intensity of around 200 W. All items must be connected into the final circuit.

⊗	Globe rated at 50 V; 25 W
⊗	Globe rated at 50 V; 25 W
⊗	Globe rated at 100 V; 150 W
	100 V battery
	100 V battery

3 marks

Chapter 13 – Magnetism

Question 1

A student is investigating fields produced by combinations of bar magnets. One combination she investigates is shown in the diagram below.

Which of the following best describes the magnetic field at point *P*?

A. It is stronger than the field due to one magnet only.
B. It is about the same as the field due to one magnet only.
C. It is weaker than the field due to one magnet only.
D. It is close to zero.

1 mark

Question 2

Which one of the following statements best describes the presence of ferromagnetism?

A. A magnet attracts a magnetic material, e.g iron.
B. A magnet creates a magnetic field in a material, e.g. plastic.
C. A magnet creates parallel magnetic alignment of neighbouring atoms in plastic.
D. A magnet creates a parallel magnetic alignment of neighbouring atoms in iron.

1 mark

Question 3

Two long straight wires are carrying current in opposite directions, as shown in the diagram below (viewed end on).

(a) Which of the following best describes the magnitude and direction of the magnetic field at a point exactly midway between the two wires?

A. The field is zero.
B. The field is greater than that due to a single wire and is directed upwards in the diagram.
C. The field is greater than that due to a single wire and is directed downwards in the diagram.
D. The field is less than that due to a single wire and could be directed either upwards or downwards in the diagram.

1 mark

(b) If the current in *one* of the wires was reversed in direction, which of the answers to part (a) would now be correct?

1 mark

Question 4

Two solenoids are connected to a source of AC electricity as shown in the diagram below. The point P is exactly midway between the two solenoids.

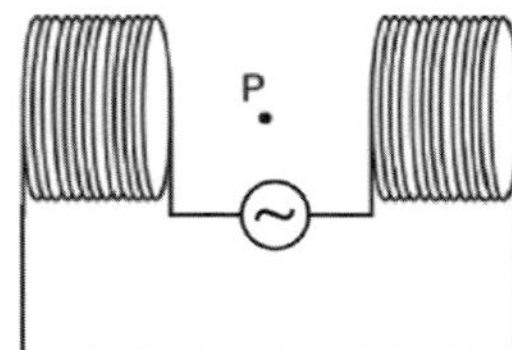

Ignoring Earth's field, which of the following best describes the magnetic field at P?

A. The magnetic field varies from left to right at the same frequency as the AC electricity.
B. The magnetic field is zero at the point P.
C. The magnetic field has a steady value and its direction is to the left.
D. The magnetic field has a steady value and its direction is to the right.

1 mark

Question 5

A small bar magnet is free to rotate about a central point, as shown in the diagram below. It is located near a solenoid. The current direction in the solenoids is shown.

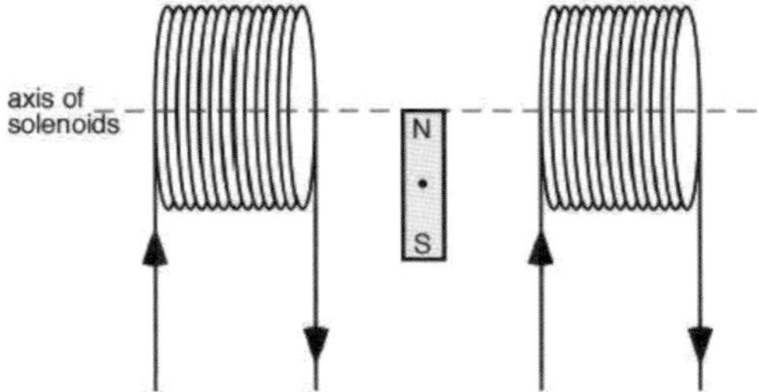

Initially the bar magnet is held so that it cannot rotate. When it is released, which of the following options best describes its motion (if any)?

A. The bar magnet does not rotate.
B. The bar magnet starts to rotate in an anti-clockwise direction.
C. The bar magnet starts to rotate in a clockwise direction.
D. The bar magnet vibrates about its starting position.

1 mark

Question 6

From the following list of metals classify those which are (ferro-)magnetic and those which are not.

aluminium, cobalt, copper, gold, iron, lead, nickel, platinum, silver, tin, titanium and zinc.

2 marks

Question 7

Two bar magnets are shown in the diagram below. One magnetic field line has been drawn.

Label the four magnetic poles in the diagram, and sketch the rest of the magnetic field around the two bar magnets, using at least six more field lines.

3 marks

Question 8

A bar magnet is shown in the sketch below. It is surrounded by a number of small freely moving compass needles, shown as circles.

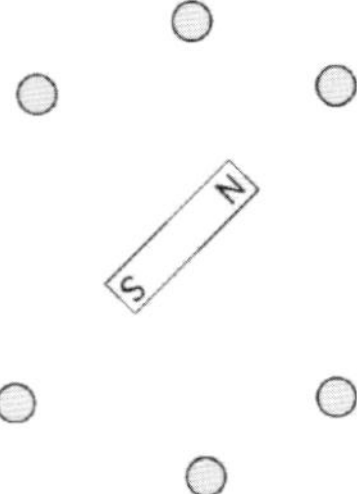

Deduce the direction of each of the compass needles. Draw a small arrow in each circle to show your deduction. You should assume that the Earth's magnetic field is not significant.

3 marks

Question 9

A small bar magnet is placed in an E–W orientation in the diagram below. At the point B, the field of the bar magnet has approximately the same magnitude as the magnitude of Earth.

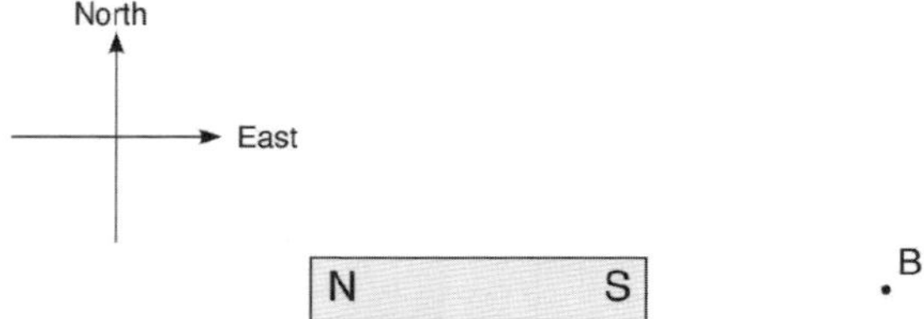

Deduce the direction of the total magnetic field at the point B. Indicate this direction by a small arrow on the diagram at the point B.

2 marks

Question 10

The pattern of Earth's magnetic field is shown in the diagram below.

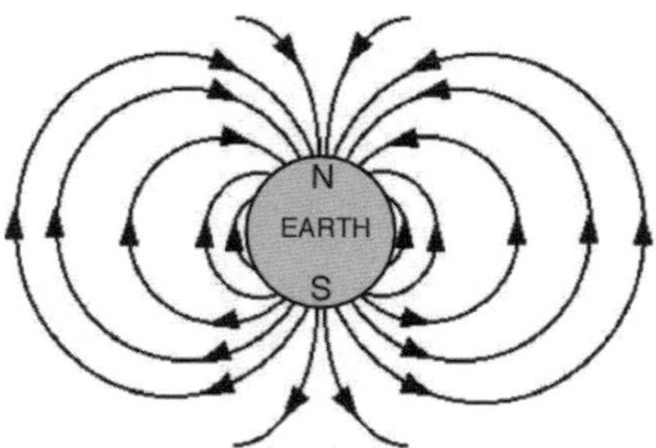

Compare the nature of the magnetic pole at the Earth's North pole with the nature of a north pole on a small bar magnet.

2 marks

Question 11

Compare the shape of the magnetic field produced by a solenoid and a bar magnet.

2 marks

Question 12

Two solenoids are aligned and facing each other. An overhead view is shown in the diagram below.

Sketch the resulting magnetic field pattern of the solenoids inside and between them, with at least four field lines.

2 marks

Question 13

Two long straight wires are carrying current in opposite directions, as shown in the diagram below (viewed from above).

Sketch the magnetic field patterns in the space around the wires in the diagram above. You should neglect any contribution from the Earth's magnetic field.

3 marks

Question 14

A wire carrying a current of 10.0 A is shown below.

• A

(a) Calculate the strength of the magnetic field produced by the current carrying wire at point A which is 5.0 cm from the wire.

2 marks

(b) Explain what would happen to the strength of the magnetic field produced by the current carrying wire if point A was placed 10.0 cm from the wire.

2 marks

Question 15

A narrow solenoid of 100 turns and length 20.0 cm carries a current of 10.0 A.

(a) Calculate the strength of the magnetic field inside the solenoid.

2 marks

(b) Explain what would happen to the strength of the magnetic field produced by the solenoid if the current is doubled.

2 marks

Question 16

Diagrams **A–G** represent possible field lines for various types of different fields (e.g. gravitational, electric, magnetic).

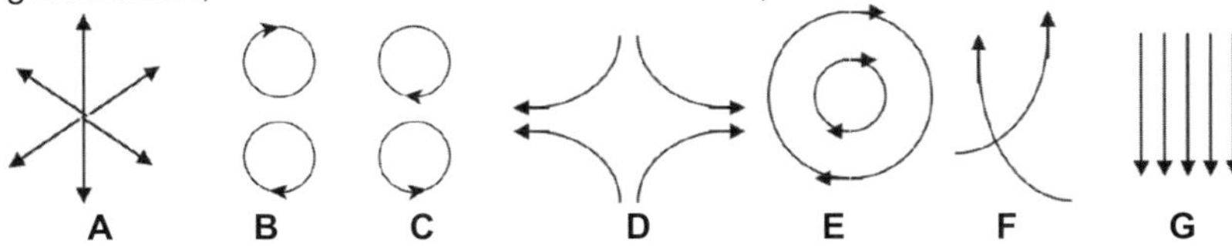

Pick which one or more of diagrams **A–G** that could represent magnetic field lines. For each choice describe a context in which this magnetic field might exist.

Answers

Chapter 1 Motion in a straight line

1 • distance is a scalar quantity; displacement is a vector quantity
• displacement is equal to the vector subtraction of the initial position from the final position, whereas distance is simply the distance traversed along the path taken from the start to the finish

2 • speed is a scalar quantity; velocity is a vector quantity
• speed is equal to the rate of change of distance (or equal to change in distance divided by change in time for the average speed); while velocity is equal to the rate of change of displacement (or equal to change in displacement divided by change in time for the average velocity)

3 Time, distance and speed are scalars; velocity and displacement are vectors.

4	D	Use $v = u + at$ and $x = ut + ½at^2$
5	A	Divide by 3.6
6a	B	Use $x = vt - ½at^2$
6b	D	Use $v = u + at$
7a	A	It stops after 2.6 s (use $v = u + gt$)
7b	D	Displacement = 0 (from definition); use distance = 2 × height
7c	B	Force of gravity always points downwards; ***F*** and ***a*** are in same direction.
8	B	Speed directly from graph; acceleration from gradient; distance from area under graph.
9	A	Gradient of graph gives speed.
10	D	Calculate distance for each train to stop ($v = 0$; use $v^2 = u^2 + 2ax$).
11a	3.0 m s^{-1}	The graph is linear from 0.0 m s^{-1} to 6.0 m s^{-1}.
11b	9.0 m	The distance is equal to the average speed × time (or the area under the graph).
11c	5.0 m s^{-1}	Read from graph.
12		

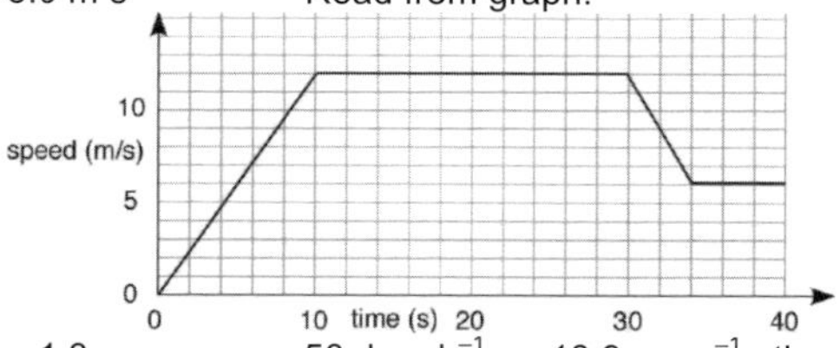

speed (m/s)
0
5
10
time (s)
0
10
20
30
40

13a	~ 1.8 s	50 km h^{-1} = 13.9 m s^{-1}; then read from graph; you will need to interpolate.
13b	39 ± 2 m	The distance is equal to the average speed × time (or the area under the graph). This is only an *estimate*; a range of answers would be acceptable.

14a

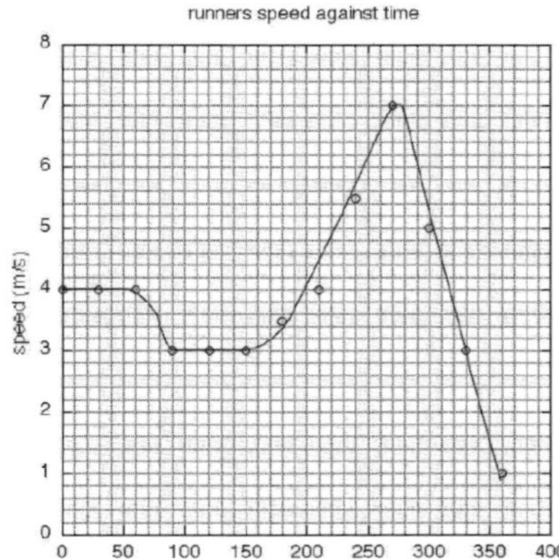

14b 240 m — Speed is constant over this time; multiply speed by time.

15a

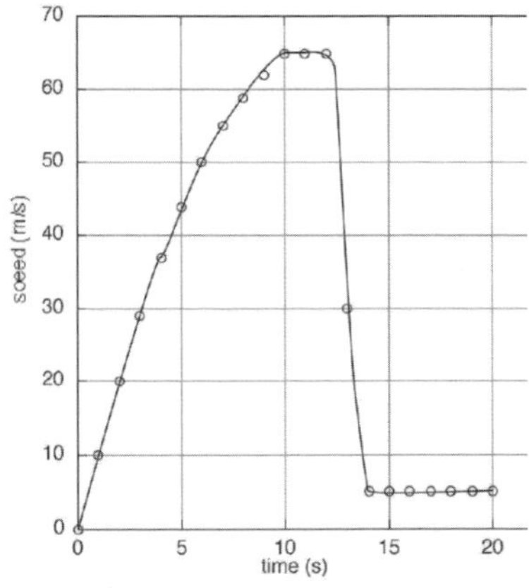

15b	65 m s^{-1}	Read from graph.
15c	5 m s^{-1}	Read from graph.
15d	650 $\pm$ 50 m	Estimate average speed and multiply by time or use area under graph.
15e	B	Read from graph.
15f	33 m s^{-1}	Average speed = distance/time
16	8.3 m s^{-1}	Average speed = distance/time
17a	2.0 mm s^{-1}	Gradient of the graph; also equal to average velocity due to linear graph.
17b	3.0 mm s^{-1}	Gradient of graph
17c	2.5 mm s^{-1}	Average velocity = displacement/time

18a The graph is symmetrical. The magnitude of the gradient at the start is the same as the gradient at the end. This implies that the velocity is the same but in the opposite direction.

18b 1.5 m s^{-1} — Average velocity = displacement/time
Direction must be positive i.e. upwards.

18c 0 m s^{-1} — The gradient of the graph at t = 10 s is zero.

18d

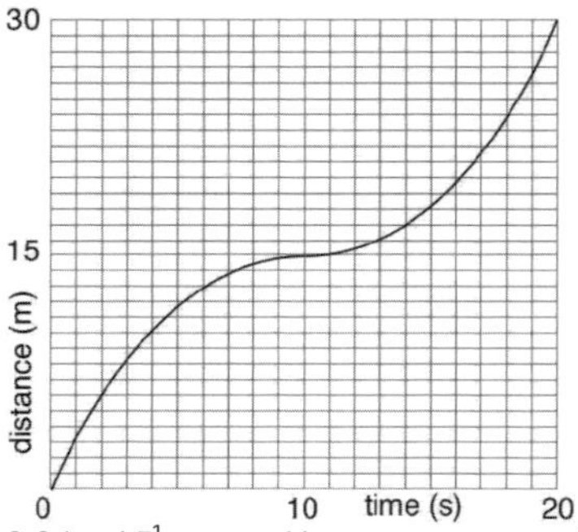

30
15
distance (m)
0
10 time (s) 20

19 8.9 km h^{-1}
2.5 m s^{-1} — Use average speed = distance/time

20a 2500 s — Total time = 500 + 1000 + 1000 = 2500 s = 42 min. (She was wearing flippers at least for the first kilometre ... the world record for 1500 implies a speed of about 1.7 m s^{-1}.)

20b 1.0 m s^{-1} — Use average speed = distance/time

20c

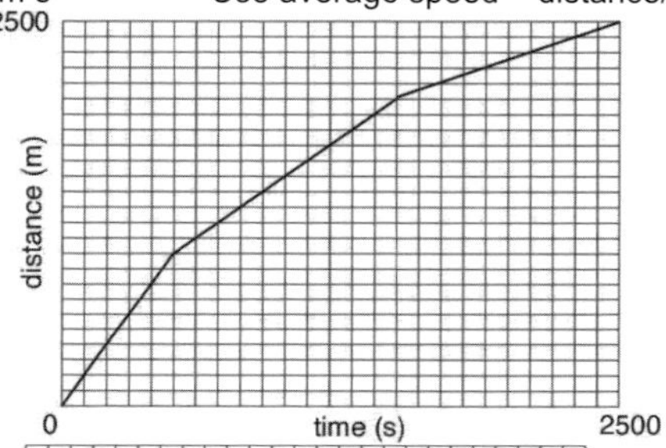

2500
distance (m)
0
time (s) 2500

20d

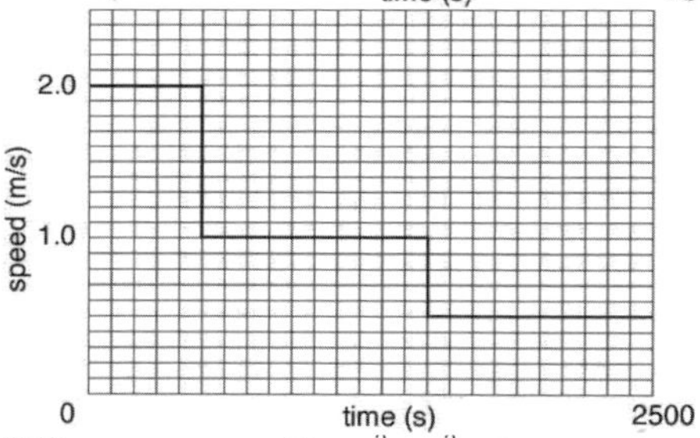

2.0
1.0
speed (m/s)
0
time (s) 2500

21a 0.82 m — Use $v^2 = u^2 + 2gs$

21b 3.7 m — Use $s = ut + ½gt^2$

22a 9.4 m s^{-2} — Use $s = ½gt^2$

22b 7.5 m s^{-1} — Use $v = u + gt$ (with $g = 9.4$ m s^{-2})

22c 11.5 m s^{-1} — Same gain in speed as Alice + an initial 4.0 m s^{-1}, or use $v = u + gt$ with $u = –4.0$ m s^{-1}.

23a 3 m s^{-1} right — Subtract the velocity of the observer (second object) from the velocity of the observed (first object); use vector subtraction.

23b 5 m s^{-1} left — Subtract the velocity of the observer (second object) from the velocity of the observed (first object); use vector subtraction.

23c 8 m s^{-1} N — Subtract the velocity of the observer (second object) from the velocity of the observed (first object); use vector subtraction.

23d 80 m s^{-1} W — Subtract the velocity of the observer (second object) from the velocity of the observed (first object); use vector subtraction.

24a Unless the air resistance is significant (unlikely unless the basketball is moving very fast) these should have the same magnitude (though opposite in direction).

24b Re-arrange $v_2 = –v_1 + at$ into $v_1 + v_2 = gt$ and hence $g = 2(v_1 + v_2)/t$.

24c The timing uncertainty will be very significant for the smaller values of v_1 *and* v_2; so use the largest possible value of these (consistent with OHS); and make many repeat measurements. Could also calculate the size of the % uncertainty to strengthen this argument.

25a	Average speed = distance over time; identify closest value of time to the final distance (10 m); it probably won't be possible to get a precise value.
25b	Find the time interval that includes the specific time, and find the average speed over that time interval ($= v/\Delta t$); again, precision is unlikely.
26a	$s = \frac{1}{2} gt^2$ (assuming that $u = 0$); make g the subject of the equation.
26b **26c**	The uncertainty of the time measurement will be ±0.2 s; the likely time Interval for a drop of 1.0 m will be close to 0.45 s, thus the uncertainty is over 40%. For the larger drop distances (e.g. $s = 5.0$ m), this reduces to close to 20%. Also the uncertainty in the length measurement will reduce. Best strategy would be to repeat the readings many times (one change) at the largest drop distance, omitting the smaller drop distances (second change).

Chapter 2 Motion on a plane

1a	A	From the definition of displacement.
1b	C	The displacement is equal to the diameter of the track.
1c	B, C, D	From the vector nature of velocity.
2	C	Change in velocity = final velocity – initial velocity (vector subtraction).
3	A, C	v_H remains constant; v_V increases from zero (vector sum must also increase).
4a	A	To find relative velocity, subtract the velocity of the observer from the observed velocity (vector subtraction).
4b	B	To find relative velocity, subtract the velocity of the observer from the observed velocity (vector subtraction).
4c	C	Draw vector triangle of situation; gives two vectors of 10 m s^{-1} at right angles; addition using Pythagoras gives 14(.1) m s^{-1}.
5a	C	To find relative velocity, subtract the velocity of the observer from the observed velocity (vector subtraction).
5b	B	To find relative velocity, subtract the velocity of the observer from the observed velocity (vector subtraction).
5c	B	Convert 54 km h^{-1} to 15 m s^{-1}; add two vectors at right angles.
6	D	'Sideways' component will steadily increase from zero value while the 'straight ahead' value remains constant.
7a	0.53 m min^{-1}	Total distance (s) = 2.10 m; $t = 4$ min; average speed = s/t
7b	150 cm	Draw vector diagram and use Pythagoras.
7c	0.63 cm s^{-1}	Average velocity = displacement/time
8a	17(.3) units	x-component = 20 × cos30
8b	10 units	y-component = 20 × sin30
8c	0	Vector $\boldsymbol{a}$ is at right angles to the *y–axis*
8d	29 units	Sum of x-components = 10 + 17(.3); total y-components = 10; now use Pythagoras
8e	20°	Draw vector triangle; $\tan\theta$ = total v_Y/total v_X = 10/27(.3)
9a	40 m s^{-1}	Vectors are at right angles; use Pythagoras to add.
9b	53°	Use $\tan^{-1}(\lvert\mathbf{b}\rvert/\lvert\mathbf{a}\rvert) = \tan^{-1}1.33$
9c	40 m s^{-1}	Same magnitude, but different direction (use vector diagram).
9d	129°	Same formula as for 10b but different vector diagram.
9e	72 m s^{-1}	Still two vectors at right angles; use Pythagoras again.
9f	69°	Similar to 10b; different values
10a	Relative to Sam: container will fall vertically; relative to observer: will follow a curved (parabolic) path from above P into the bin.	
10b	0.78 s	Time for container to fall will equal time for Sam to move from P to Q; use $s = \frac{1}{2}gt^2$.
11a	1.4 m up	Read from diagram.
11b	3.7 m	Add 1.4 and 3.4 using Pythagoras.

11c 3.1 m s^{-1} Use $v = s/t$ for horizontal motion.

11d 6.7 m s^{-1} Use $s = ut + ½gt^2$ with $t = 1.1$, $g = –9.8$; $s = +1.4$

11e 7.3 m s^{-1} Use Pythagoras to add vertical and horizontal components.

11f 65° Use $\tan\theta = v_V/\text{total } v_H$

12a The motion of the boat will be affected by two forces – the boat's motor and the flow of the river. These vector quantities add to produce motion that moves the boat downstream as well as across the river, as shown in the diagram.

12b Consider just the motion of the boat perpendicular to the riverbank; use $v = s/t = 100/11.5 = 8.7$ m s^{-1}.

12c 5.0 m s^{-1} The velocity of the boat in still water added to the river flow velocity are at right angles and form a right-angled triangle with an angle of 30° between the resultant velocity and a perpendicular to the bank; now use tan30 = $v_{RIVER}/8.7$.

13a 5.7° Use the vector diagram shown to deduce $\cos\theta = 199/200$.

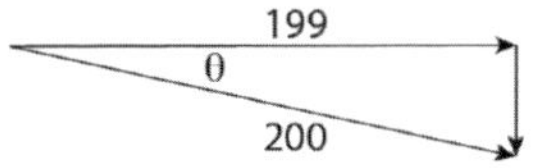

13b 20 m s^{-1} Use Pythagoras on vector diagram shown for 14a.

14a 2.8 m s^{-1} Plane airspeed adds to crosswind to form right-angled vector triangle; new speed = 72(.8) m s^{-1}; increase = 2.8 m s^{-1}

14b 16° Use $\tan\theta = 20/70$ from vector diagram below.

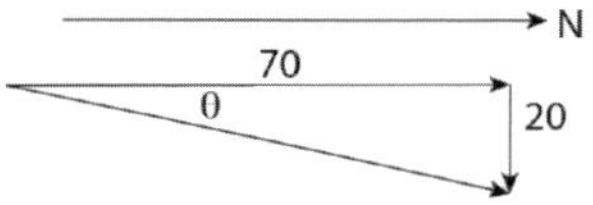

14c 17° Use $\sin\theta = 20/70$ in new vector diagram below.

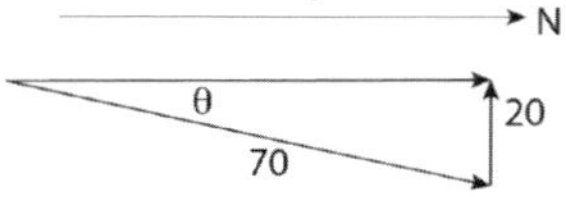

Chapter 3 Forces, acceleration

1	D	This is classic Newton I.
2	A	This is classic Newton I.
3a	D	Lift must balance the weight (= 392 000 N).
3b	A	If $a = 0$ then the net force is zero.
4	D	This follows from definition of mass and weight.
5a	A	Runners and walkers use friction to maintain or accelerate forward motion.
5b	50	Newton's third law
5c	B	Use $F_{NET} = ma$
6a	D	Friction opposes the tendency to relative motion.
6b	A	Net force must = 0; hence sum of the other forces must be upwards.
7	A	Net force = 0; hence friction force on wheels must be forward.
8a	B	Only force after leaving the bat is gravity.
8b	C	Air resistance opposes the motion through the air.
9	C	When the ball was in contact with the ground, the friction opposed the relative motion between the ball and the ground.

10 The weight (mg) of the ball will be downwards and exactly equal in magnitude to the upwards force of air resistance on the ball (Newton I).

11

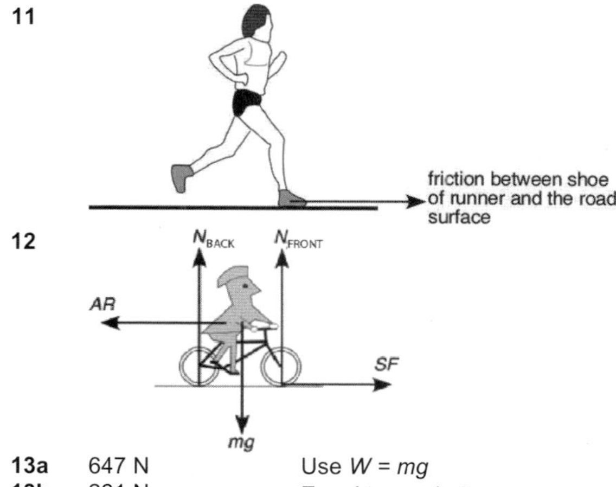

12

13a 647 N — Use $W = mg$

13b 221 N — Equal to $mg\sin\theta$

13c The vector sum of all the forces acting on him = zero.

13d 608 N — Equal to $mg\cos\theta$

13e 221 N — The friction balances the component of his weight down the slope.

14 He is not accelerating because the net force on him (and bike) = 0; the force forward (friction between driving wheel and road) is equal and opposite to retarding forces of rolling friction and air resistance.

15a 65 kg — Use $W = mg$

15b 0 N — Newton I

15c 365 N — Equal to the component of her weight down the slope.

15d 5.6 m s^{-2} — Use $mg\sin\theta = ma$

16a
- up the slope: friction
- vertically down: weight
- perpendicular to the slope: normal reaction force

16b 0 N — Newton II: if $a = 0$ then $F_{NET} = 0$

16c 553 N — Must balance $mg\sin\theta$

16d There would be a net force acting on him of 553 N pointing straight down the slope.

16e 9.2 m s^{-2} — Use $F = ma$

17 *Situation 1*: net force > 0; $a > 0$; friction forward between tyres and road minus air resistance and rolling friction backwards.

Situation 2: net force = a = 0; friction forward between tyres and road equals sum of air resistance and rolling friction.

Situation 3: net force > 0; $a > 0$; component of weight down the slope minus air resistance and rolling friction backwards up the slope.

Situation 4: net force > 0; $a > 0$ (both directed to the centre of the circular path); friction sideways towards the centre of the circular path is unbalanced; other horizontal forces are balance (friction between tyres and road forwards (tangentially)) and sum of rolling friction and air resistance backwards (tangentially).

Situation 5: net force > 0 and backwards; $a > 0$ and backwards; friction backwards between tyres and road plus air resistance and rolling friction backwards together are the net force.

Situation 6: net force = a = 0; friction up the hill between tyres and road equals component of weight of car down the hill.

18 At this point the total gravitational field = 0, so the weight = 0, but the mass is unchanged.

19a 242 N — Use $mg\sin\theta$

19b 746 N — Use $mg\cos\theta$

19c 242 N — Normal force balances the component of weight perpendicular to the slope; the only force left is the component of the weight down the slope.

19d 3.0 m s^{-2} — Use $F_{NET} = ma$

20 415 N — Components of the two tensions upwards add to $2T\sin 50 = 637$

21 3064 N — Friction force total must balance the vector sum of the tensions (this is equal to $2T\cos 40$).

22
- the person must be accelerating upwards
- net force upwards must be greater than mg
- hence normal reaction force > mg
- after the person has left the ground, the normal reaction force vanishes

23a

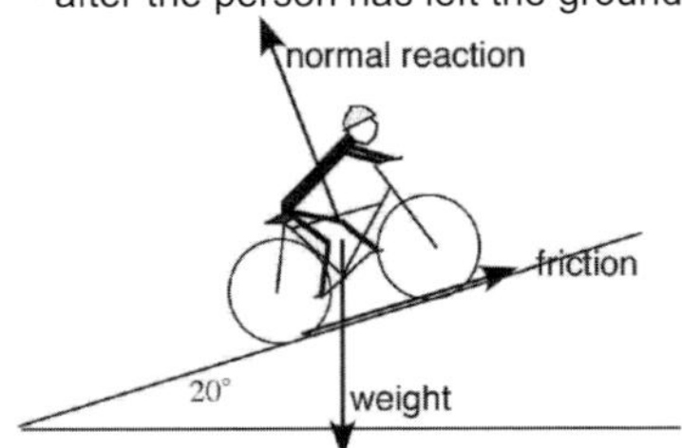

(Some students may add in *rolling friction*, which points in the opposite direction to the static friction up the slope.)

23b 0 N — Newton's first law

24a 820 N — Use $F_{NET} = ma = 300 = 1120 - F_{RETARDING}$

24b 680 N — F_{NET} now becomes $F_{BRAKES} + 820 = ma = 1500$

25a 1000 N — Use F_{NET} (on the trailer) $= ma$

25b 2500 N — Use F_{NET} (on the car) $= ma = 1500 = F_{DRIVING} - 1000$

25c 2500 N — The driving force is supplied by this friction force.

Chapter 4 Forces, energy

1a B — Calculate KE before and afterwards.

1b B — Loss of KE means that the collision is inelastic.

2a D — The human body is about 25% efficient in this regard.

2b C — P = work/time.

3 C — 25% of 1200 W = 300 W; work done = power × time

4 D — Calculate mgh; divide by 0.9

5a C — Use $P = Fv$

5b A — $F_{NET} = 0$ (no acceleration); gravity component down slope = 2500; hence 2700 – 2500 = 200 N

5c D — Total energy = 50 kW × 3600; then divide by 0.2

6a C — Net force = 0; therefore $T = mg \times \sin\theta$

6b D — Use $\mu N = \mu mg\cos\theta$

7a D — Use $mgh \times 12$

7b D — Divide answer to previous question by 30 ($P = W/t$)

8a C — $N = mg\cos\theta$

8b A — Newton's first law

8c C — Solving $Fr = \mu N = \mu mg\cos\theta$ and $Fr = mg\sin\theta$ gives $\mu = \tan\theta$

9a 6.3 J — Calculate KE at finish and subtract KE at start.

9b 'Missing' energy transformed into other forms (primarily thermal energy).

10a 30 000 J — KE = $\frac{1}{2} mv^2$

10b 22 m s^{-1} — Use KE + GPE (total energy at top of the hill) = KE at bottom of hill.

10c 53 kJ (52.8) — Use $0.5m(v^2 - u^2)$

10d 20 MJ — Total chemical energy used must be 4.0 × 5 MJ (from efficiency).

11
- work done = Fs
- if cadence is doubled with the same force, then twice the work is done in the same time
- hence power is doubled

12 91% — Use $\frac{1}{2}(m + M)5^2 - \frac{1}{2}(m + M)1.5^2$; then use a ratio to original KE.

13 The work done in stopping the car must be equal to both the original KE and also the product Fs; hence $Fs = \frac{1}{2} mv^2$. Hence, if F is the same, the distance s (the stopping distance) should increase as the square of the speed.

14a
- for the first 5 s the driving force is > than the rolling friction
- this gives a net force which will result in a + acceleration ($F = ma$)
- the net force starts at 50 N and steadily decreases to 0 N at 5 s
- the initial acceleration will also steadily decrease

14b	875 J	Area under graph
14c	292 W	$P = W/t$
14d	750 J	Work done against friction is $F \times s$ where F is the rolling friction.
14e	3.2 m s^{-1}	Total work done = 125 J = KE gain
15a	6000 J	GPE = mgh
15b	20%	Efficiency = energy out/energy in
15c	167 W	$P = W/t$ (convert 3 min to 180 s)
16a	750 ± 10 J	Area under graph
16b		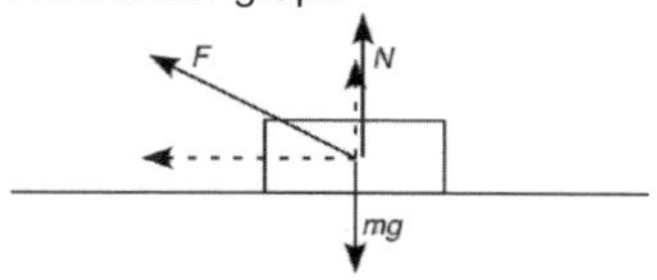 • the amount of friction depends on the size of N, i.e. how firmly the surface of the floor and the box are being pressed together • the upward component of F tends to *reduce* the size of N
17a	1200 J	GPE = mgh
17b	80 W	Power = GPE/time
17c	400 J	All the GPE is converted into KE
18a	200 000 J	Work done by net force = change in KE
18b	5 m	Use KE = GPE (after converting 36 km h^{-1} into m s^{-1})
19a	4.55×10^4 J	GPE = mgh
19b	4.55×10^4 J	All GPE converts to KE
19c	4.48×10^4 J	At the 'stopping point' he has lost 44 800 J of GPE and has no KE. Hence, elastic PE must be = 44 800J.
20a	39 m	$150 \times \sin 15$
20b	39 kJ	GPE = mgh
20c	15 m s^{-1}	$0.3 \times$ GPE = $0.5mv^2$
20d	181 N	70% of GPE = $Fr \times 150$
20e	0.19	Divide answer to previous question by $mg\cos\theta$
21a	4000 J	Calculate KE = $0.5mv^2$
21b	16 m s^{-1}	Vector subtraction of velocity
21c	2560 J	= change in KE = $0.5 \times m \times (10^2 - 6^2)$
22	432 kJ	$E = P \times t$
23a	1.4 N	Use $P = Fv$
23b	20 N	Use $P = Fv$
23c	96 N (95.5)	Use the component of the weight down the slope ($mg\sin\theta$).
23d	18(.3) kW	Total power output = 200 + 14 + 96 = 310; multiply by 60
24a	4000 N m^{-1}	Use EPE = $0.5kx^2$
24b	Linear between (0,0) and (1.5 m, 6000 N)	

Chapter 5 Momentum, energy, simple systems

1a	A	Calculate p before and afterwards; must be conserved.
1b	B	Calculate KE before and afterwards.
1c	B	Loss of KE means inelastic.
2a	B	KE before = $12.5(M + m)$; after = $1.125(M + m)$; ratio = 91%
2b	A	Impulse = $m \times \Delta v$
3a	A	Conservation of momentum ($45 \times 1 + 55 \times 5 = 320$; divide by 100)
3b	C	Momentum is always conserved, but KE decreases here.
3c	C	$F_{NET} = 0$ (no acceleration); gravity component down slope = 2500.
4a	A	Use conservation of momentum.
4b	D	Use impulse = $\Delta p = m \times \Delta v$
4c	B	Use impulse = $\Delta p = m \times \Delta v$
5a	A	Use conservation of momentum: $1.2 \times 3 + 0 = 3.6v$.

5b	D	Can be solved combining KE and momentum conservation (laborious) but easier to observe that A, B and C all violate momentum conservation. Can then check KE conservation.
6a	50 kg	Find *v* from $v^2 = 2as$; then use $p = mv$. Answer is to 2 sig figs.
6b	2.3 kJ	Easiest to use $E = p^2/2m$
6c	The momentum has been transferred through the mats to Earth; the KE has been transformed into other forms, including thermal energy and sound energy.	
7	28 m s^{-1}	Use impulse $(F\Delta t) = m\Delta v$
8a	14 m s^{-1} upwards	Vector subtraction ($\boldsymbol{v}_{FINAL} - \boldsymbol{v}_{INITIAL}$)
8b	5.6 N s	Use impulse $(F\Delta t) = m\Delta v$
8c	70 N	Use impulse = $F\Delta t$
8d	5.6 kg m s^{-1} downwards momentum is transferred through the floor to Earth; same amount is transferred upwards to the ball. This follows from Newton 3.	
9	The momentum has been transferred through the ground to Earth.	
10a	56 N s	Use impulse $(F\Delta t) = m\Delta v$
10b	They have the same magnitude but are in opposite directions.	
11	Use $F\Delta t = m\Delta v$ in the form $F = m\Delta v/\Delta t$; as Δt increases, *F* decreases	
12	Injuries are caused when large forces act on the human body (second collision); they keep moving forward because of inertia. Such forces can be reduced by lengthening the time taken by the second collision (from $F = m\Delta v/\Delta t$).	
13	Crumple zones increase the time taken for collisions to occur; this reduces *F* from the relationship $F = m\Delta v/\Delta t$.	
14a	2.5 m s^{-1}	Momentum afterwards must equal momentum beforehand.
14b	The accelerations are given by $a = \Delta v/\Delta t$; since Δv is greater than in the smaller car, and Δt is the same, the passengers in the small car will have larger decelerations. This could mean greater injuries (from $F = ma$).	
15	63 m	The key relationship is work done $(Fs) = \Delta$KE; hence $s = mv^2/2F$. So stopping distances will be proportional to v^2.
16	11 m	The key relationship is work done $(Fs) = \Delta$KE; hence $s = mv^2/2F$. So stopping distances will be proportional to v^2. (This is a 19% reduction.)
17a	25 m s^{-1}	Use $F\Delta t = m\Delta v$ to find $v_{INITIAL}$
17b	KE is transformed to elastic PE (EPE) in the spring until the KE is zero, then the EPE is transformed into the KE of the car until the EPE is zero.	
17c	Momentum of the car is transferred into the spring barrier and hence to Earth; then momentum is transferred from Earth through the spring barrier to the car in the opposite direction.	
18a	14 m s^{-1}	Use horizontal component of momentum only: $20m = 2mv\cos 45$.
18b	Elastic	KE before $(0.5 \times m \times 400)$ = KE afterwards $(2 \times 0.5 \times m \times 200)$
18c	They exert equal and opposite impulses on each other in the vertical directions, since total vertical momentum is zero throughout the collision.	
19a	A: elastic B: inelastic	Ball A strikes the floor at 14 m s^{-1} (from $v^2 = 2gs$) and rebounds at the same speed (hence same KE); ball B loses all its KE.
19b	A: 28 m s^{-1}; upwards B: 14 m s^{-1}; upwards	Use vector subtraction of velocities ($\boldsymbol{v}_{FINAL} - \boldsymbol{v}_{INITIAL}$)
19c	A: 112 N B: 56 N	Use impulse = $F\Delta t = m\Delta v$
20a	39 m	Net force on skydiver = 4410 – 90*g* = 3528 N; hence $a = -39.2$ m s^{-2}. Now use $v^2 = u^2 - 2as$ to give *s* = 38.6 m
20b	6.2 kN s	Find *t* from $v = u + at$, then use impulse $F\Delta t = m\Delta v$ with $F = 4410$ N
20c	The vertical momentum starts from 0 then increases downwards (Earth gains an equal amount of upwards momentum); when he contacts the net, his momentum is transferred to Earth through the net and its supports. The total momentum of the skydiver-Earth system remains at zero throughout.	
21a	N: 7.5 kN s W: 10 kN s	The total momentum before equals the total momentum afterwards.
21b	12.5 kN s	The total momentum before equals the total momentum afterwards; use Pythagoras.

21c 37° (N of W)

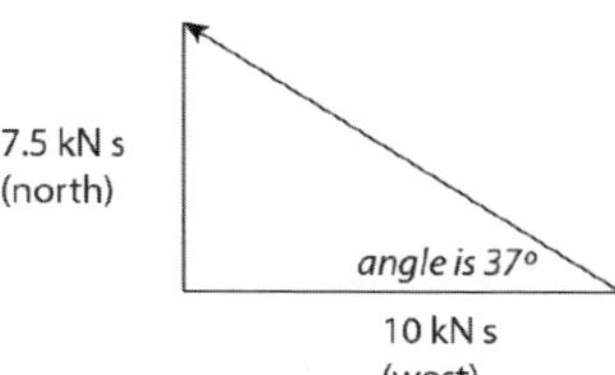

21d Inelastic
Speed after collision = momentum (12 500) ÷ mass (17 500) = 7.1 m s^{-1}
KE before collision = $0.5 \times 750 \times 10^2 + 0.5 \times 1000 \times 10^2$ = 87.5 kJ
KE after collision = $0.5 \times 1750 \times 7.1^2$ = 44.1 kJ
Hence change is KE is a loss of 43.4 kJ

Chapter 6 Wave properties

1 Mechanical waves require a medium in order to transport their energy from one location to another. A mechanical wave is not capable of transmitting its energy through a vacuum.

2 B C — Standard knowledge

3 0.78 m — Use $v = f\lambda$

4 1.2×10^{10} Hz — Use $v = f\lambda$

5 200 m s^{-1} — Use $v = f\lambda$

6 Sound waves: 3; Waves in a guitar string: 1; Ripples in a pond: 2; Waves on the surface of a drum: 2.

7 An example of a transverse wave is an electromagnetic wave, where electric and magnetic fields vibrate perpendicular to the direction of propagation of the wave; in sound waves in air, by contrast, air particles vibrate parallel to the direction of propagation of the wave. All longitudinal waves are mechanical waves; by contrast, transverse waves need not be mechanical – for example, electromagnetic waves.

8 (a) the particles: the arms of spectators moving vertically
(b) particle motion: transverse
(c) wavelength: tricky to measure unless there is more than one 'pulse' – if there is, then the wavelength is the distance between adjacent pulses
(d) the period (assuming more than one pulse) would be the time between pulses at one location
(e) speed: measure distance travelled divided by time taken

9 C — This is the only option *particularly* associated with wave motion.

10
- water particles oscillate vertically
- a graph of their displacement with time would be a sinusoidal graph
- adjacent water particles are slightly out of phase with each other
- the amount that they are out of phase varies in a regular fashion
- this results in the wave maintaining its shape as it travels

(other approaches with diagrams are also possible)

11a D — From the definition

11b C E — From the definition

11c C — This is the 'best' answer

12a Amplitude = 1.3 m; Wavelength = 8.0 m — From the definition

12b A — The other options would have the wave shape not in the same position; option A means that two whole wavelengths will have passed.

12c 0.67 m s^{-1} — Use $f = v/T$

13a C — From the definition; F is nearly at a compression but not quite.

13b A — From the definition

14 Sound is an example of a longitudinal wave. Energy is transferred from the source to the kinetic energy of the vibrating air particles. This energy is passed on to neighbouring air particles until the vibrations reach the receiver of the sound. The vibrations are parallel to the direction of motion of the sound wave.

15 A water wave (in a regular swell in the ocean) is an example of a transverse wave. The amplitude is *half* the vertical distance between the crests of the swell and the troughs.

16 C — The key point is the lack of need for a medium.

17 3.1(2) m — Use $f = v/\lambda$

18 2.0(1) rad.m^{-1} — Use $k = 2\pi/\lambda$

19 There are many possibilities. One would be infra-red electromagnetic waves, such as those generated by a wood fire, and used for keeping people nearby warm. The very hot burning logs generate electromagnetic waves, which then move through the surrounding air until they are absorbed by the skin or clothes of the nearby people. The energy of the electromagnetic waves is then transformed to thermal energy, keeping them warm. Another one would be microwaves (in domestic kitchens).

20 There are many possibilities. One would be the sound waves generated by a loudspeaker at a railway station. The loudspeaker converts electrical signals carrying information into sound waves, which then travel through the air to the ears of people waiting to catch a train. The sound waves are then converted to electrical signals containing the information in the listener's hearing system.

21a Water

21b Normally air (unless travelling through another medium such as water)

21c The material of the Earth

22a

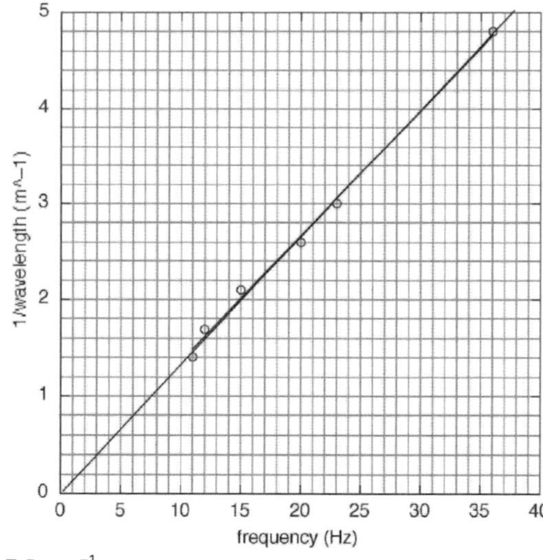

22b 7.5 m s^{-1} — Rearrange the equation $v = f\lambda$, with $(1/\lambda)$ as the subject. This gives $1/\lambda = (1/v)f$; hence the gradient of the graph above is equal to $(1/v)$.

22c The form above gives a linear graph, and it is easy to measure the gradient, which then gives a measure of $1/v$. Plotting f against λ gives a curved graph (a hyperbola), and it is more difficult to get data from this graph to calculate v.

23a 1.5 m — From the definition of amplitude

23b 12 m — From the definition of wavelength

23c 0.13 Hz — Period must be 7.5 s (two complete wavelengths); $f = 1/T$.

23d 1.6 m s^{-1} — Speed is distance/time (or $v = \lambda/T$)

23e Less energy — The amplitude is less than the previous waves.

Chapter 7 Wave behaviour

1a A, B — Both patterns show reflection of the waves off a plane barrier.

1b C — The waves change direction (refract) as they move from shallow to deep water at the interface.

1c D — The waves diffract as they go through the small gap.

2	A	The waves reflect off the surface of the TV satellite dish to a focal point.
3	C	Foghorns diffract sound waves over wide angles.
4	D	Superposition – positive pressures created that cancel out the equivalent negative pressures of noise waves and vice versa.
5	A	A surfer catches a progressive or travelling wave.
6	C	Extra energy is added in time with the natural resonant frequency of the swing – resonance.

7a

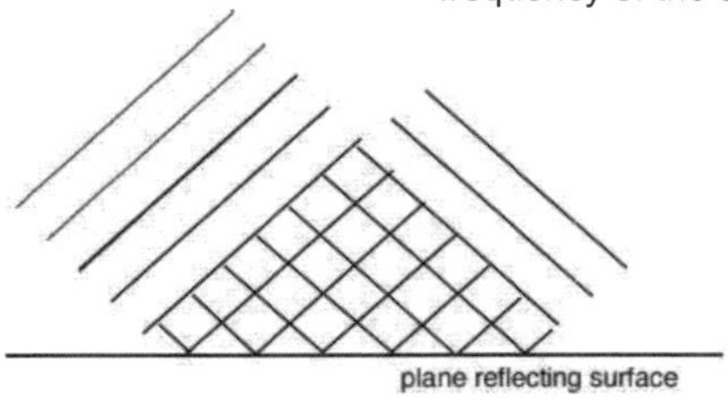

plane reflecting surface

7b

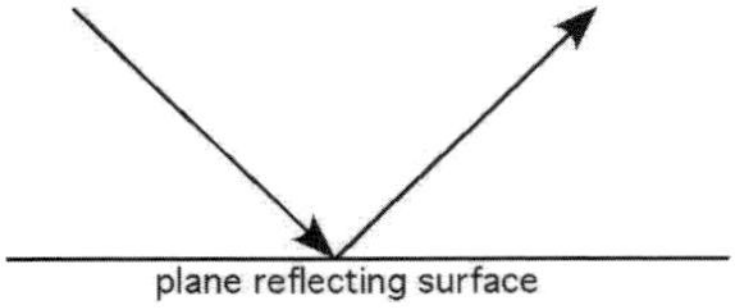

plane reflecting surface

8a

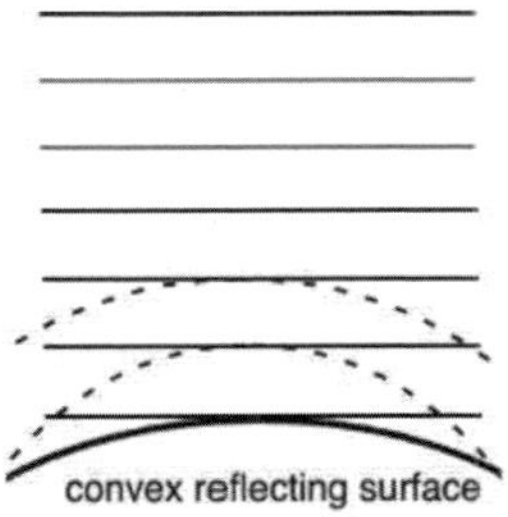

convex reflecting surface

8b

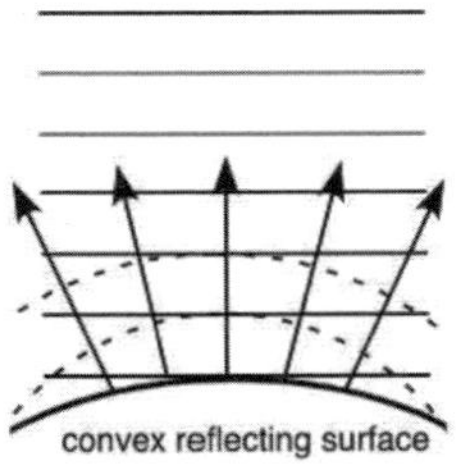

convex reflecting surface

(only the reflected rays are shown; the incident rays are all parallel and vertically downwards)

9a

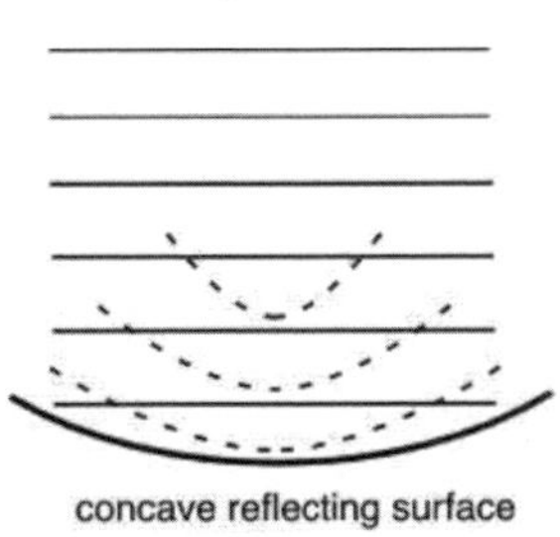

concave reflecting surface

9b

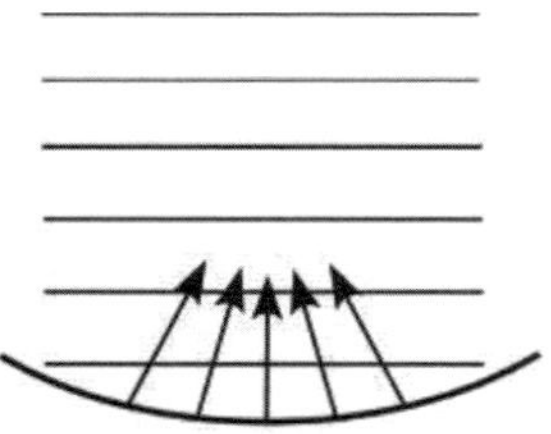

(only the reflected rays are shown; the incident rays are all parallel and vertically downwards)

10

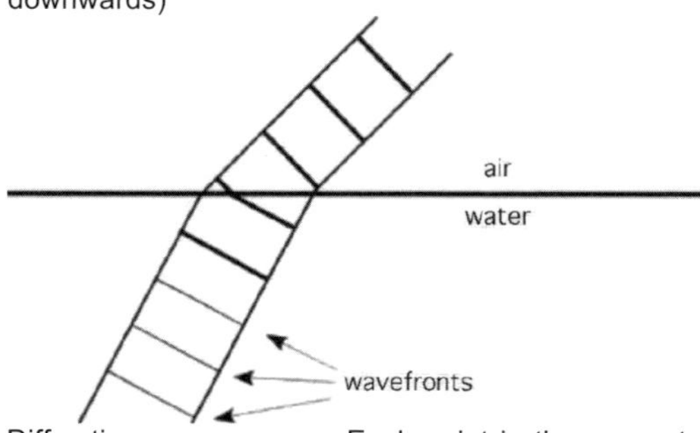

11 Diffraction

Each point in the gap acts as a single point, emitting circular waves.

12

- when the waves enter the shallower water, they slow down
- this is analogous to light entering a medium of higher refractive index
- they bend 'towards the normal'; that is, become more parallel to the beach
- the frequency of the waves is unchanged, but both the wavelength and the speed are decreased

13a 0.5 s later

13b 1.0 s later

14a 0.5 s later

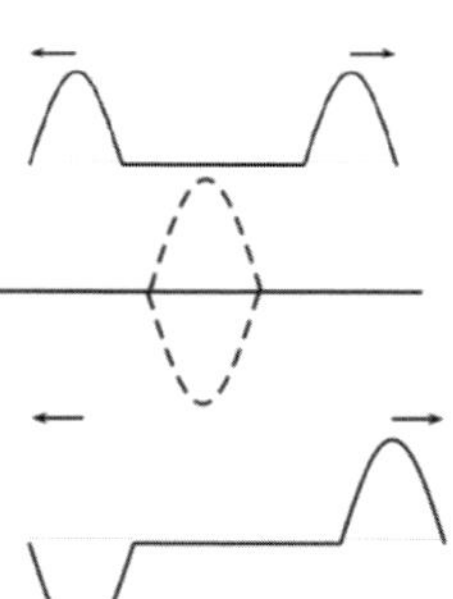

14b 1.0 s later

15a X

Diagram X shows a progressive wave travelling to the right.

15b Y

Diagram Y shows a standing wave oscillating up and down.

15c The dashed line shows the wave one quarter of a period (*T*/4) later.
The wave has moved one quarter of a cycle to the right.

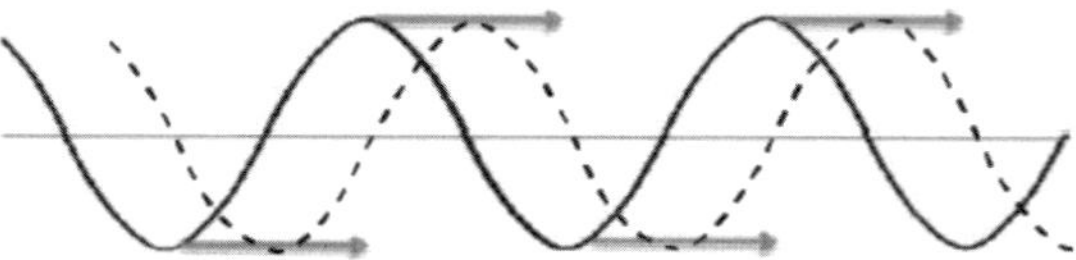

15d	The dashed line shows the wave one quarter of a period (*T*/4) later. The wave has moved one quarter of a cycle up from the bottom and down from the top hence giving a straight line.	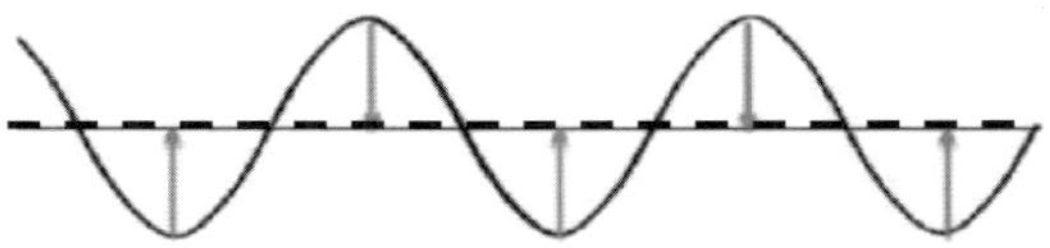
16a	Driving frequency	Driving frequency is the frequency of the driving force. The driving force is an external force applied to the oscillating system (e.g. parent pushing child on swing).
16b	Natural frequency	Natural frequency of the system is the frequency at which it will vibrate freely (frequency of vibration after a single push by parent).
16c	Amplitude of the motion	The amplitude of the motion is the displacement of the vibration from its position at rest to its maximum displacement. If the driving frequency is the same as the natural frequency, the amplitude will increase (e.g. parent synchronising pushes with natural frequency of the system).
16d	Energy transfers/transformations	Energy is transferred from the driving force mechanism to the oscillating system (e.g. parent's push to child on swing). In the oscillating system, energy is transformed from kinetic energy to potential energy (e.g. in a child's swing from maximum kinetic energy at zero amplitude displacement to maximum gravitational potential energy at maximum amplitude displacement).
17a	Break step	By breaking step instead of marching the soldiers were intending to **not** create any unwanted resonances in the bridge structure.
	Spread apart	By spreading apart the soldiers were intending to **not** concentrate any oscillatory driving forces generated on a particular section of the bridge.
17b	Driving forces	The two driving forces were the strong wind and the unintended synchronisation of the soldiers' footsteps.
17c	Energy transfers	Wind energy and soldiers footsteps' energy into the resonant frequency oscillations of the bridge structure.
18a	Resonance	Blowing air across the bottle also forces some extra air into the bottle and the pressure builds up. Eventually the pressure builds up so much that some air is now pushed out of the bottle. The fast moving air blowing across now sucks air out of the bottle until the pressure is low enough to suck more air back in. This creates the vibration or resonance.
18b	240 Hz	Half full bottle
	480 Hz	Three quarter full bottle
18c	Air columns	By adding water to the bottle there is less air space available so it takes less time for the pressure to build up. This means the vibrations happen more quickly and so produce a higher resonant frequency. Half the air column in the bottle doubles the original resonant frequency. One quarter the air column in the bottle quadruples the original resonant frequency.

Chapter 8 Sound waves

1	B	B is true while A, C and D are all incorrect.
2	D	From the definition
3	A	The higher the pitch the higher the frequency.
4	B	resonance
5	A	Follows from the inverse square law

6	D	The back and forth motion creates compressions and rarefactions which propagate as a longitudinal wave.
7a	D	Horizontal vibrations push the candle flame back and forth.
7b	B	A longitudinal wave
8	D	Louder means larger amplitude vibrations, and lower in pitch implies a reduced frequency.

9a

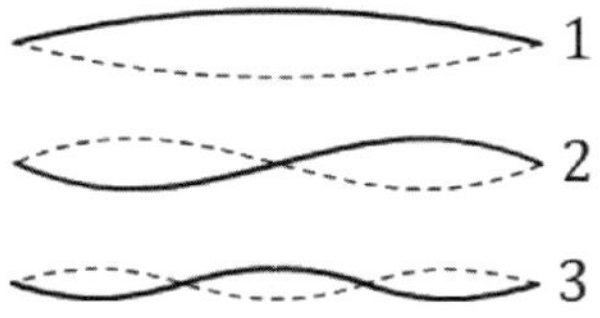

1
2
3

9b	1.20 m	$\lambda/2 = 0.60$ m
9c	$3\boldsymbol{f_0}$	See diagram above in answer to 9a.

10a Sound reflects off the sound barrier so that no sound reaches the houses in a direct line (a diagram could be used as well.)

10b Sound diffracts around the sound barrier so that some sound energy reaches the houses (a diagram could be used as well).

11a	0.50 m	$v = f\lambda$
11b	0.25 m	Fundamental frequency ($\boldsymbol{f_1}$) occurs with $\lambda/2$ in the pipe.
11c	1336 Hz	$\boldsymbol{f_2} = 2\boldsymbol{f_1}$
11d	The pipe is too short.	A resonant frequency of 334 Hz would imply $\lambda = 1.00$ m and hence for a fundamental frequency ($\boldsymbol{f_1}$) the pipe length would need to be $\lambda/2$ or 0.50 m long.
12a	0.18 W m^{-2}	Inverse square law (0.40 W m^{-2} $\times$ (4 $\times$ 9)
12b	6.32 m	Inverse square law (2.0 m $\times$ $\sqrt{10}$)
13a	3	A rarefaction is a region of pressure less than average atmospheric pressure.
13b	4 ms	The wave repeats itself every 4 ms.
13c	250 Hz	The frequency is the reciprocal of the period ($1/T$).
13d	1.34 m	Use $f = v/\lambda$.
13e	A	From the definition of amplitude
14	69 Hz	The wavelength (from the graph) is 5 m; now use $f = v/\lambda$.

15

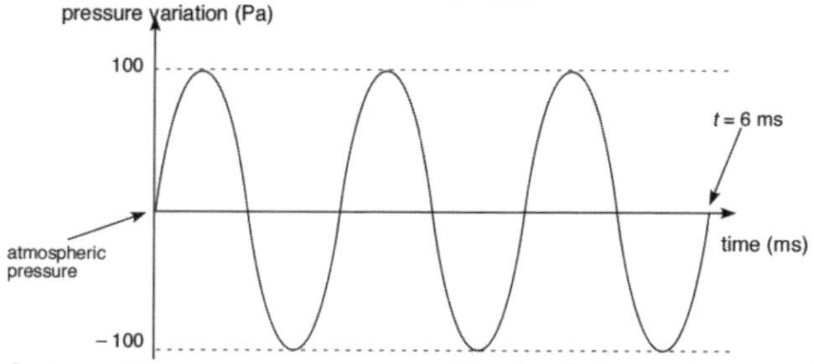

pressure variation (Pa)
100
$t = 6$ ms
atmospheric pressure
time (ms)
– 100

16	Superposition	The fourth image is caused by the addition of the displacements of the two original pulses when they overlap. This is the principle of superposition.

17 The dashed line shows the result of superposition.

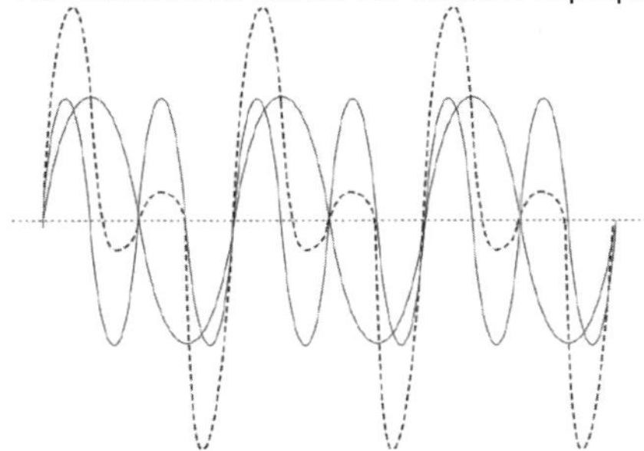

18 B and C combine to form A; simply look at one or two points (where they are not all zero!)

19a	240 m s^{-1}	km h^{-1} ÷ 3.6
19b	300 m s^{-1}	km h^{-1} ÷ 3.6
19c	lower	The waves are arriving further apart, and less frequently.
19d	10.00 kHz	Use the Döppler effect formula: $f' = \frac{v + v_0}{v - v_S} f_0$ f_0 is the original frequency, v_S the speed of the source, v_O the speed of the observer and v the speed of sound.
19e	14.00 kHz	Use Döppler effect formula.
19f	240 m s^{-1} to the right	By travelling at the same speed as the jet, the wave fronts are now arriving normally.

20a The tuning fork on the right (**B**) will resonate at the same 256 Hz frequency.

20b	(i) Lower frequency	The extra mass of the Blu Tack will cause the tuning fork to vibrate at a lower frequency.
	(ii) 254 Hz	$f_{\text{beat}} = \lvert f_2 - f_1 \rvert$ and tuning fork **B** has a lower frequency
21a	423 m s^{-1}	$v = \lambda f$ (wavelength is 1.08 × 2 m)
21b	282 Hz	$v = \lambda f$ (wavelength is now 1.5 m.)
21c	>196.0 Hz – higher	10% extra weight increases tension in the string thus increased the speed of the wave in the string which increases the frequency ($f = v/2L$).
21d	<196.0 Hz – lower	The greater linear density of the double bass string decreases the speed of the wave in the string which decreases the frequency ($f = v/2L$).

22
- you would clap your hand at time $t = 0$
- you would measure the time until the echo from the bottom of the well reached you
- this time consists of two parts – the sound travelling down and the sound travelling back up to you
- now use distance = speed × time (where time would be *half* the total time measured above)

23	345 m s^{-1}	Use speed = distance/time (where distance = 1000 m)

24
- he will hear a series of echoes
- the first echo will be from the nearest step
- there will then be a succession of echoes at regular intervals
- the time between successive echoes will be quite short (t = 2 × step width/speed of sound)
- the total effect might be something like a 'chirp'

Chapter 9 Ray model of light

1	B	It is always virtual and diminished.
2	A, C, D	It can be magnified and virtual, diminished and real, and magnified and real.
3	B	It is always virtual and diminished.

4 A, C, D — It can be magnified and virtual, diminished and real, and magnified and real.

5 A — A convex mirror gives a wide field of view.

6 C — A concave mirror collects parallel rays from a distant astronomical object and focuses them at a point; the small image formed is then magnified.

7 A — This is the definition of refractive index.

8 A, C and D — These are the two laws of plane reflection.

9 A and D — Standard knowledge.

10a

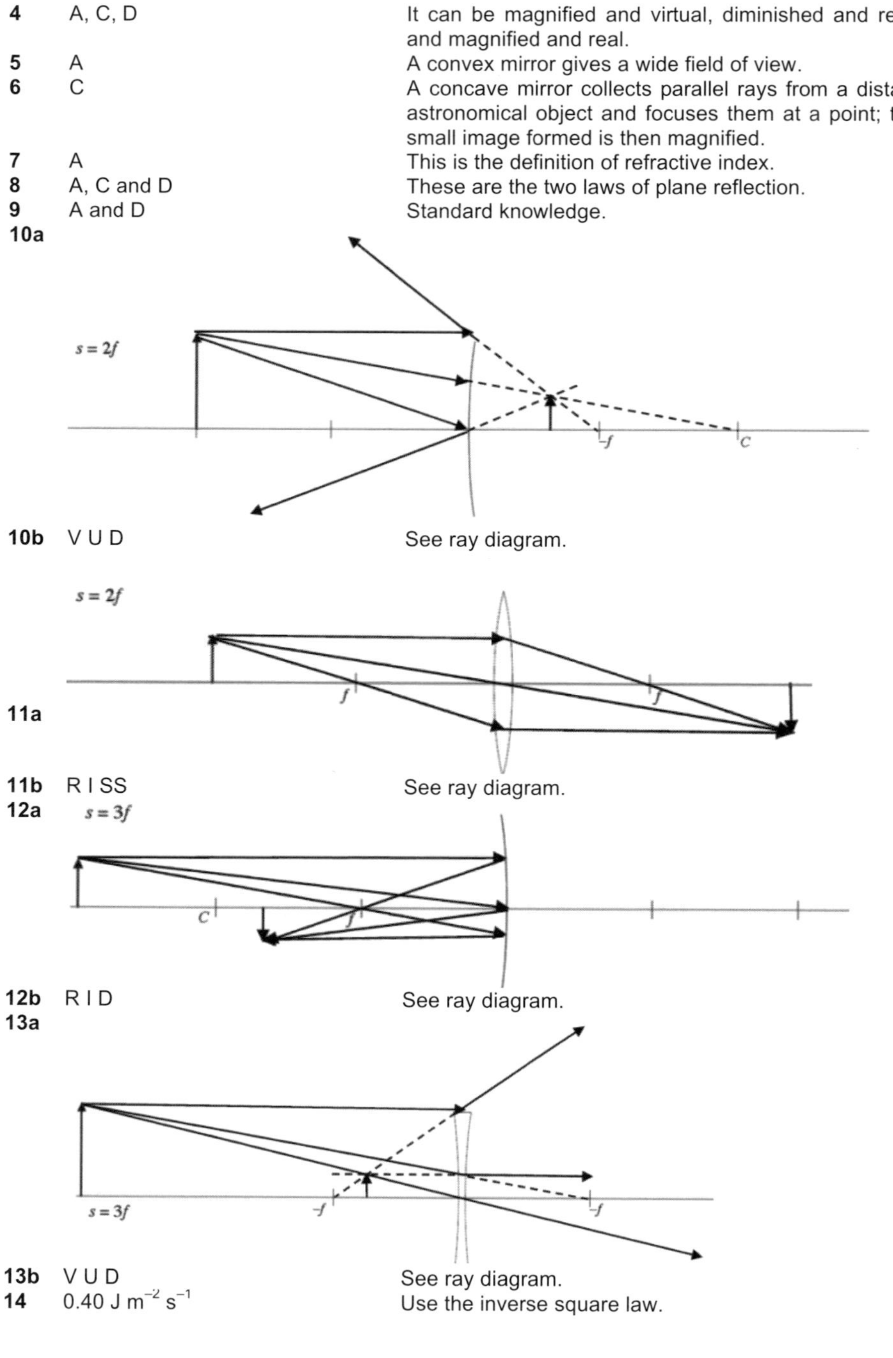

10b V U D — See ray diagram.

11a

11b R I SS — See ray diagram.

12a

12b R I D — See ray diagram.

13a

13b V U D — See ray diagram.

14 0.40 J m^{-2} s^{-1} — Use the inverse square law.

15 1.3 — Angle between normal and ray at X is 50°; now use Snell's Law.

16 1.40×10^8 m s^{-1} — Use $c_M = c_V/n_M$; (M = medium, V = vacuum)

17 1.24×10^8 m s^{-1} — Use $c_M = c_V/n_M$; (M = medium, V = vacuum)

18a Red is refracted the least, green next and blue refracted the most.

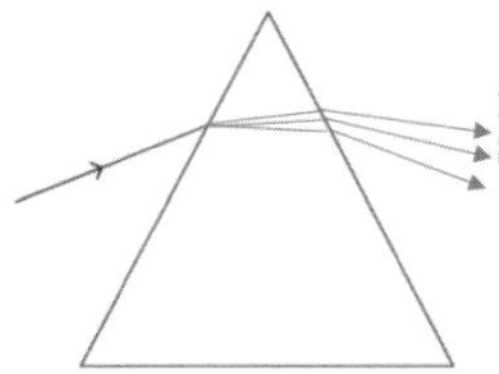

18b Dispersion

18c Refractive index (n) of glass is different for different colours of light. — e.g. $n_{RED} = 1.48$, $n_{GREEN} = 1.50$, $n_{BLUE} = 1.52$

18d Water droplets in the rainbow have a slightly different refractive index for water for each colour in the dispersion of the sunlight: the droplets reflect the colours back to the viewer at slightly different angles.

19 1.39 — Because the graph is plotted with the refracted angle on the y-axis, the gradient will give the inverse of the relative refractive index; since the surrounding medium is air, with n = 1, this is very close to the absolute refractive index. The gradient (of the trend line – *not* of individual points) is equal to 0.72, so n = 1.39.

20

(a) 2.50×10^8 m s^{-1} — (a) use $c_M = c_V/n_M$

(b) 6.67×10^{14} Hz — (b) frequency from $f = v/\lambda$

(c) 6.67×10^{14} Hz — (c) frequency is the same in plastic as in air

(d) 375 nm — (d) the wavelength is reduced by the factor of the refractive index

21

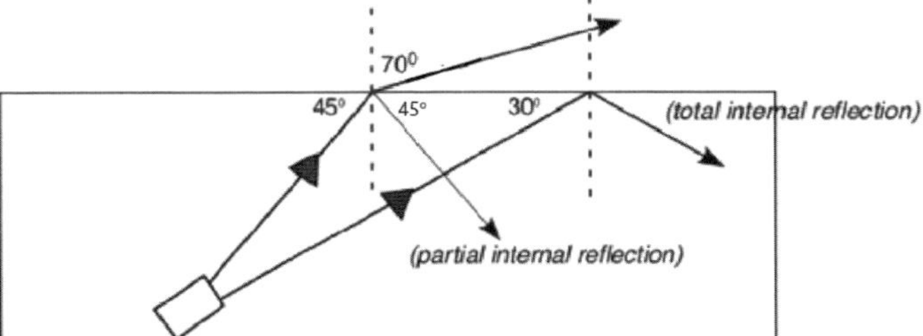

(use Snell's Law to calculate the angle into air and the critical angle = $\sin^{-1}(1/1.33) = 48.8°$)

22

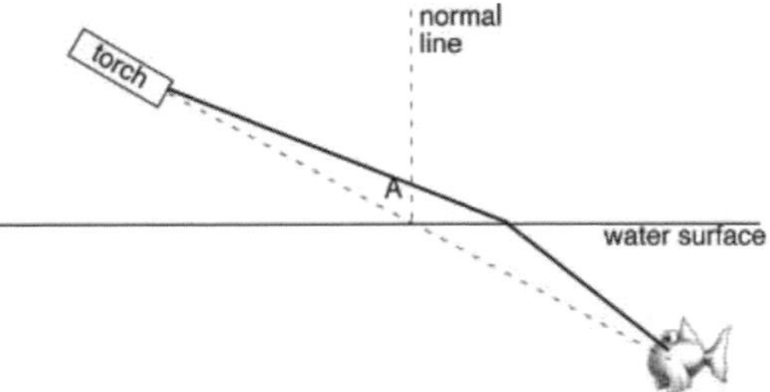

The approximate correct light ray is shown as a solid line. When the light enters the water from the air, it bends towards the normal, as shown by the solid line.

23a 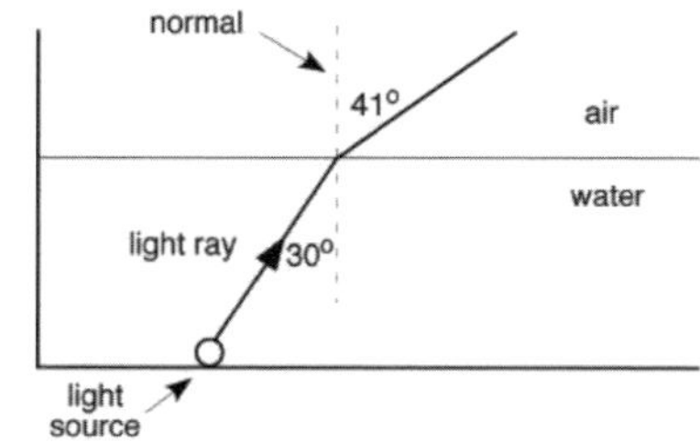

(the calculation using Snell's Law gives 40.5°)

23b 50° — Use Snell's Law; assume n_{AIR} = 1 and angle of refraction is 90°.

24 1.48 — Use Snell's Law; assume I = 64° and that r = 90°.

25a 23° — Use Snell's Law.

25b a = 38° (reflection)
c = 23° (alternate angles)
d = 23° (reflection)
e = 38° (ray will emerge at the same angle that it entered, since block has parallel sides)

25c 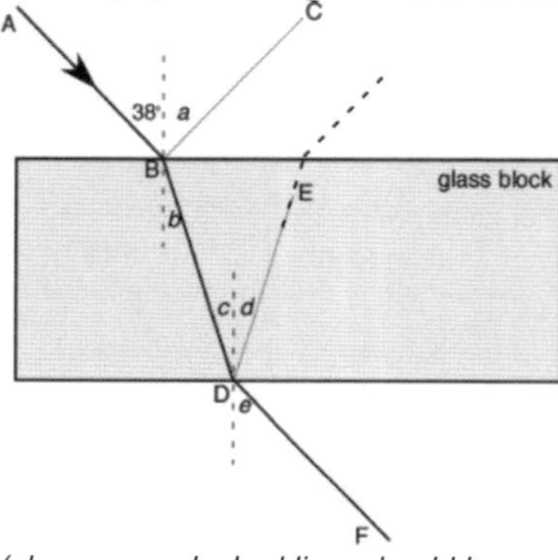

(shown as a dashed line; should be parallel to line BC)

25d D — The higher refractive index of blue light will cause greater refraction; hence b will be less.

26 D — The four critical angles are (in order): 41.8°, 42.3°, 37.6° and 35.0°.

27a Cladding must have a smaller refractive index than core, so total internal reflection can occur.

27b When the fibre bends it is still possible for total internal reflection to occur, provided the bend is small. If the incoming rays are nearly parallel to the fibre axis, this makes it possible for fibre to have greater bending and still maintain total internal reflection (hence minimising losses).

28a Speed in diamond/speed in seawater = 0.54.

28b Frequency ratio = 1 : 1.

28c Wavelength in diamond/wavelength in seawater = 0.54.

29 1.367 kW m^{-2} — Use the inverse square law.

30 *The Invisible Man* has to have the same refractive index as his surroundings to be invisible – so in air he must have n = 1.00. If he eats visible food (an apple say), it has to become invisible instantly or else we would see it travel down to his stomach (and perhaps further). As his eyes have the same refractive index as air, he will not be able to focus the light onto his retina – so the invisible man is blind. He would also have to wear clothes with n equal to that of air.

Chapter 10 Thermodynamics

1a C — Add 273 to the Celsius measure.

1b A — Subtract 273 from the Celsius measure.

2 B — From the definition of thermal equilibrium

3 F T T F T F F F

4 B — There will be thermal equilibrium between the cup of coffee and its surroundings.

5 D — Use $\Delta Q = mc\Delta T$; 100 m^3 of water has a mass of 100 000 kg.

6 B — Use $\Delta Q = mc\Delta T$

7 B — Use $Q/t = kA\Delta T/d$ with k as the subject

8 B — From the definition (or use $k = (Q/t) \times d/(A\Delta T)$)

9 C — Apply ratios to $Q/t = kA\Delta T/d$; assume ΔT is the same for both.

10 A, B C & D
- the larger the ΔT is, the faster the transfer rate
- the longer the pipe, the slower the rate
- the thicker the pipe, the faster the rate
- materials vary in their *thermal conductivity*

11 When two bodies are in thermal equilibrium, they are at the same temperature, measured by a (reliable) thermometer *or* there is no net transfer of thermal energy from one to the other when they are in thermal contact and at equilibrium.

12 600 J kg^{-1} — Use $Q = mc\Delta T$

13 5189 kJ — Add $mc\Delta T$ and mL = 4520 + 669 (kJ)

14 315 K — Heat gained by ice = $0.015 \times 336000 + 0.015 \times 4182T$
Heat lost by water = $0.1 \times 4182(60 - T)$; equate and solve.

15 When steam contacts a cool hand – say at 37° C – it will transfer both latent heat of vaporisation (2260 kJ/kg plus 4.18 kJ /kg per degree of cooling; water at 100°C will only transfer the second quantity).

16 At seaside locations, there is a large mass of water nearby with a high specific heat; it takes longer to heat in the summer, and convection effects often cause sea breezes (a convection diagram would be useful here).

17 21 cents — Total energy required (kJ) = 334×2 (melting) + $2 \times 100 \times 4.18$ (heating water) + 2×2260 = 6860 kJ = 6.86 MJ; cost is 21 cents

18 The methylated spirit will quickly warm towards its boiling point (low mass, lower specific heat than water, low BP) then evaporate (volatile); evaporation removes a good deal of thermal energy from your hand (latent heat of vaporisation).

19a 'High thermal mass' is equivalent to 'high heat capacity' (*mc*); so high values of *c* and high values of *m* would both contribute. There will be trade-offs. For example, wood has a high *c* (1700 J/kg/K) but low density; but brick, with much higher density has *c* values around 840 J/kg/K).

19b To heat up from cold they would require more energy (*Q*) but when heated would cool down more slowly.

20 Soup with lots of solids would mean a lower proportion of water; hence a lower specific heat, so would warm and cool more quickly.

21 273 K — Water and ice must be at the same *T*; hence 273 K.

22 The first section is ice warming to 273 K (gradient is proportional to the specific heat of ice, 2.03 kJ/kg/K); the next flat section is the ice changing phase to water, the next sloping section is water warming (steeper gradient because water has a higher specific heat than ice, 4.18 kJ/kg/K), then the change of phase to steam, then the steam warming (again a lower specific heat than water, 2.10 kJ/kg/K). The phase change sections are flat because the input energy (Q) is all going into changing the phase (breaking inter-molecular bonds).

23 Wind removes the evaporating molecules rapidly from the surface of the wet material, allowing more molecules to evaporate. The washing will be cooler as a result, having lost the more energetic molecules.

24 Water on the skin will cool you down when it evaporates, as the evaporation takes significant energy (Q) from your body. However, if there is no breeze or it is humid, this process will be much slower.

25a Hypothermia is the lowering of your body's core temperature to dangerously low values (below about 35°C); this will occur if the cooling of the body is faster than its ability to heat itself; evaporative cooling from the skin cools the body very effectively.

25b Hyperthermia is the raising of body core temperature to dangerously high values (above around 38°C); cooling by evaporative methods is very effective in reversing this.

26 Water has a very high specific heat, and a fairly high density, so it is ideal for increasing the heat capacity of the house, and hence its 'thermal mass'. However, it is expensive to locate in the walls without the possibility of leaking, and imposes significant lateral pressures on containers.

27 When the room is above the temperature of the environment (the other side of the walls of the room), thermal energy is conducted through the walls at a rate proportional to the temperature difference. At first this difference is not great so the rate of thermal energy loss is small. However, as the room warms up the rate of loss increases until it reaches equilibrium where the thermal energy loss is equal to the thermal energy input from the heat pump. At this stage, the temperature reaches its maximum value.

28a 15 kW At equilibrium, thermal energy supplied from heater equals therma energy lost through walls = $kA\Delta T/d$.

28b 18°C Rate of energy loss is proportional to the temperature difference; hence this increases to 18°C.

29
- conduction transfers energy through cup walls and into air at top of cup
- convection currents in air at sides of cup and at top transfer energy upwards
- evaporation at top of cup transfers energy from coffee into water vapour in surrounds
- radiation occurs at infrared wavelengths from walls and top of the cup

30
- the end of the spoon in the hot tea becomes hot (higher temperature)
- the atoms and free electrons at that end vibrate and move randomly more energetically than before
- the energy of these movements are transferred along the spoon by collisions with nearly atoms, raising the temperature
- this process continues along the spoon

31a Glass is a poor insulator, but the air in the gap (or argon, or a vacuum) is a very good insulator.

31b Argon has lower conductivity than air (not on the course, but interesting, and is more viscous, so there is less convection in the gap; a vacuum is even better (but expensive to build reliably).

31c A large gap would allow more convection to take place, increasing energy loss

32
- the down feathers 'puff' up the material, including a thicker layer of air; air is an excellent insulator
- the down feathers reduce convection within the material, also reducing energy transfer

33a Radiation (microwaves) raise the temperature of water molecules within the food.

33b Infrared radiation falling on the bread is converted to thermal energy.

33c Conduction from the hot surface of the frypan heats the eggs.

33d The fan operating forces convection around the oven from the gas or electric heating element, transferring thermal energy to the cake.

33e First, conduction from the heating element into the water raises its temperature; convection currents are then set up transferring thermal energy throughout the water in the kettle.

34 Mittens have a smaller surface area than gloves, so conduction from the warm hands to the cold air is less.

35 The copper on the saucepan bottom is a very good conductor of thermal energy, so energy is conducted quickly and evenly over the bottom of the saucepan.

36 Air near the heater becomes hotter and less dense, hence it rises. Away from the heater it gradually cools and becomes more dense, so falls again. In this way, a 'convection cell' is set up around the room, as shown in the diagram.

37 Natural convection cells (see previous question) can become more efficient if a fan is used to 'force' the movement of air (hence 'forced convection').

38 During the day (assuming sunny) the land heats up more quickly than the sea (due to lower specific heat). Hence air over the land rises, setting up a convection cell.

39 When the fan is on, rapid convection makes most parts of the oven at the same temperature; this is good for some types of cooking.
When fan is off, natural convection (slower), and top of the oven is generally considerably hotter than the bottom. This is good for other types of cooking.

40 Assuming that the lid is on, there are no evaporation losses. The vacuum in the walls of the flask mean there can be no conduction through the walls of the flask, or convection in the walls of the flask. There will be some radiation from the outside walls and the lid, but if these are shiny and white, this also will be minimised.

41 The inside starts to warm when infrared and visible radiation enters through windows and is absorbed. Materials inside the car re-radiate, at a much longer wavelength. This is reflected back into the car because the glass windows block the longer wavelengths. The temperature keeps rising until equilibrium is achieved.

Chapter 11 Electrostatics

1	C	Electrons are removed from your jeans by the rubbing and therefore leave a net positive charge.
2a	B	The total charge on the two spheres is zero.
2b	C	Due to electrostatic induction, the charge on sphere A will be negative leaving sphere B positive.
3	B	Equipotentials are perpendicular to the electric field.
4	B	No work is done travelling along an equipotential.
5	Static electricity. Electric shock. Moist air.	When you walk on an acrylic carpet, your body can build up a charge of static electricity. The insulating soles of your shoes prevent discharge through your feet. Touching the metal doorknob with your bare fingers allows charge to flow giving you a small electric shock. When the weather is humid, the low moisture in the air makes it harder to build up a large static charge.

6 The water molecules have a permanent dipole: the negative side is attracted to a positively charged rod and is closer to the positively charged rod than the positive charges. Thus the attractive force is greater than the repulsive force.

7 Positive charge concentrates on the narrow end (small radius of curvature); hence electric field strongest there.

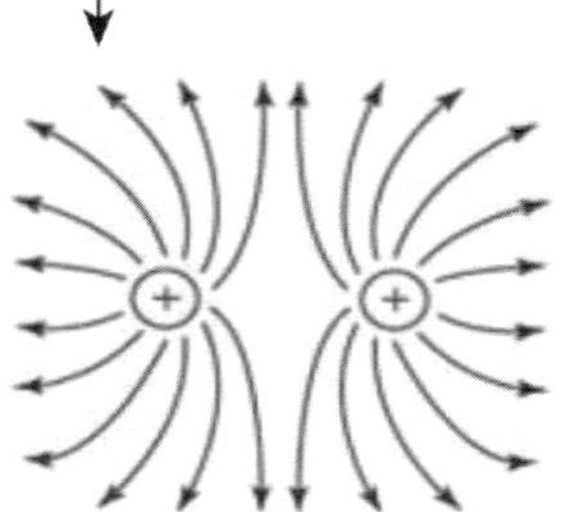

8a Two positively charged spheres with equal charges (+Q and +Q).
Note symmetry of the electric field lines.

8b Two charged spheres with 2Q and –Q.
Note asymmetry of the electric field lines.

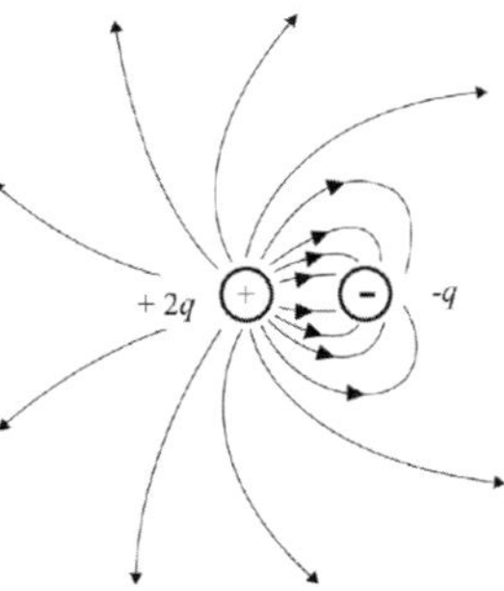

9a

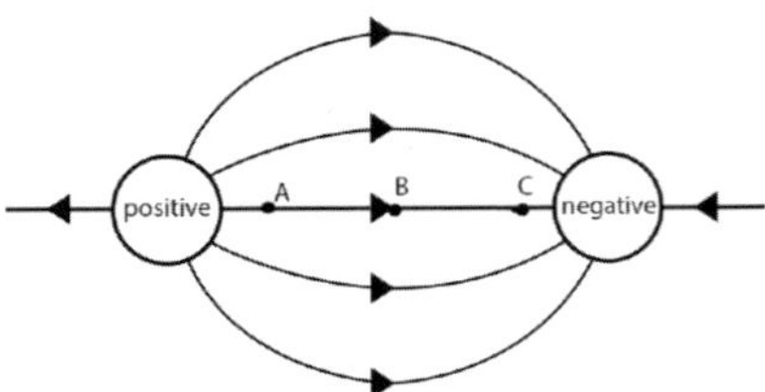

9b The fields at A and C will be in the same direction and equal in strength (symmetry argument). The field at B will also be in the same direction but weaker than the other two (field lines are less closely spaced).

9c The field at B would reduce to zero.

10a 3.6×10^{-7}N — Substitute into $F = k\frac{Q_1 Q_2}{r^2}$

10b Repulsive — The electric force between the two charges is repulsive as like charges repel each other.

10c Increase by $\times$ 4 — Inverse square law; distance has halved.

11a 4.0×10^{-6} N — Same charges, same distance, same force.

11b 5.7×10^{-6} N at 45° NW — Use Pythagoras ($a^2 = b^2 + c^2$) and vector diagram.

12a

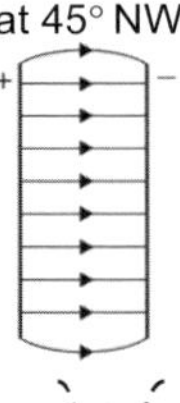

12b

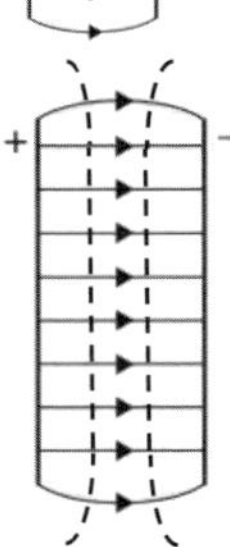

(dashed lines are equipotentials)

12c 2.00×10^5 N C^{-1}. Use $F = qE$. Force (opposite to direction of the electric field) is to the left.

12d The alpha particle will experience double the force that the electron experiences, in the opposite direction.

12e The small charge must be positive, since the force is in the same direction as the electric field. Size of the charge is given by $F/E = 9.6 \times 10^{-19}$ C (E is still = 2.0×10^5 V m^{-1})

13a 400 V m^{-1} — Use $E = V/d$

13b 6.4×10^{-17} N — Use $F = qE$

13c	3.2×10^{-18} J	Use $\Delta U = qV$
13d	3.2×10^{-18} J	KE = ΔU
13e	200 V m^{-1}	Voltage same, distance doubled so E is halved.
13f	3.2×10^{-17} N	Same q, E is halved so F is halved.
13g	3.2×10^{-18} J	KE = $\Delta U = qV$ and q and V are the same.

Chapter 12 Electric circuits

1a	Coulomb	Standard knowledge
1b	Volt	Standard knowledge
1c	Ampere	Standard knowledge
1d	Watt	Standard knowledge
1e	Joule	Standard knowledge
2	All are correct	To check, reduce to base SI units or use standard formulas ›.g. $R = V/I$)
3	D	In metals, electrons are free to move throughout the lattice of molecules.
4	C	Charge per second = $6.3 \times 10^{18} \times 1.6 \times 10^{-19}$ divided by 10.
5	A, B, C	The more free electrons, the greater the current; the larger the electronic charge, the greater the current; the faster the electrons move, the greater the current. The density of the metal is irrelevant.
6	C	More current will be drawn and hence a shorter battery life.
7	C, D	This follows from $E = Pt$ and $E = VIt$
8	B	Use $V = IR$
9	C	Amperes × hours are units of charge ($Q = It$). 1 A h is equal to 3600 C.
10	A	There are 8 lights sharing the 240 V in series, hence 30 V. Total power output is 160 W from 8 lights, hence 20 W.
11	B	Resistance depends on the material (here unchanged); the length (here increased ×4); the cross-section area (here decreased by ×4). The effect of the length increases resistance by ×4, and reducing the cross-section area also increases the resistance by ×4.
12	A, C	Lower temperatures mean less collisions of the moving electrons; shorter conductors also mean less less collisions.
13	111 ohm	Either use the formula or work out the total current (one at a time): then use $V = IR$
14	120 V	Use $P = V^2/R$.
15	24 ohm	$P = V^2/R$
16	43.2 MJ	Use $E = VIt$ (convert 24 h into seconds)
17	9.0 A	Use $E = VIt$ (convert 104 kW h to J first)
18a	4.5 A	Easiest way is to use $E = I^2Rt$
18b	240 W	$P = E/t$
19	188 W	Calculate R first (from $P = V^2/R$); then use the formula again.
20	6.25×10^{19} excess electrons (just divide 10 by 1.6×10^{-19})	
21	600 C	Use $Q = It$
22	6.5×10^{7} C	Use $Q = It$
23	0.16 ms	Use $Q = It$
24	The students would need to graph the voltage against the current and look for deviations from a linear relationship. They could monitor the ratio V/I. If this increases, the resistance is increasing; if it decreases, the resistance is decreasing.	
25	1.6×10^{18} ions s^{-1}	The current is made up of *both* electrons and positive ions. Assuming that they are in equal numbers means that the ions contribute 250 mA to the current. Hence $n = 0.250/1.6 \times 10^{-19}$.

26a Other placements are also possible, but the ammeter must be in series and the voltmeter must be in parallel with the conducting material.

26b

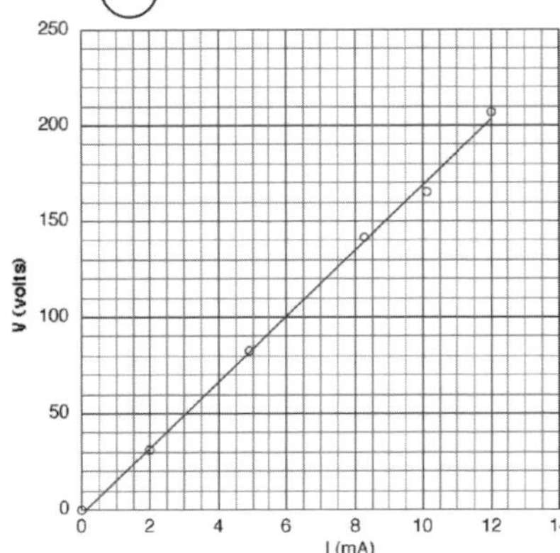

26c 41 ohm — The gradient can be used here because the conducting material is clearly ohmic (the ratio of *V*/*I* does not change in the data range).

27 0.73 — Resistance at 6 V = *V*/*I* = 1.71 ohm; at 12 V = 2.35 ohm.

28 The key reason is that metals have a large number of free electrons/m^3. For example, copper has around 10^{29}. Plastic materials have many fewer, possibly as few as 10^7 m^{-3}.

29a 4.8 J — From the definition of potential difference

29b 7.2 J — 12 J are available to each coulomb through the resistor network; if 4.8 J is lost in resistor 4 then the remainder must be lost in resistor 1.

29c 2.4 J — Because resistors 2 and 3 are in parallel with resistor 4, they must use 4.8 J between them; hence each resistor uses 2.4 J.

29d 12 J — From the definition of potential difference

30a If either headlight is ON, the corresponding warning light should also be ON, but if the headlight fails, the warning light will go OFF, due to the series configuration.

30b Headlights are connected in parallel so that:
- they receive the same voltage
- if one headlight fails, the other can still operate

30c 4.0 A (the same as the current through one headlight)

30d 0.5 V (12 V shared between headlight and warning light)

30e 0.13 ohm (0.125) — From *V* = *IR*

31
- one resistor will carry 1.0 A (from *V*+ *IR*)
- two in series will carry 0.5 A (double the resistance)
- two in parallel will carry 1.0 A each – hence 2.0 A (half the resistance)

32
- all appliances receive the same voltage (a standard voltage)
- when one fails (goes 'open' circuit) the others can continue to operate
- when one is switched off, the others can continue to operate

33a
- maximum: 150 mA (total *R* is 100 ohm)
- minimum: 50 mA (total *R* is 300 ohm)

33b
- across the 100 ohm resistor: 15 V (when other resistor is at 0 ohm)
- across the 0 – 200 ohm variable resistor: 10 V (when it is at 200 ohm)

34 Ammeters are designed to measure the current in a circuit without affecting the circuit. To measure the current, the current needs to pass through them (they are connected in series). If they do not have a very low resistance, they will affect (change) the circuit.

35 Voltmeters are designed to measure the potential difference between any two points in a circuit without affecting the circuit. To measure the potential difference, they are connected in parallel. If they do not have a very high resistance, they will affect (change) the circuit because current will be diverted through them.

36a Resistors I and II are in series; resistors III and IV are in parallel.

36b Current through resistor I = 1.0 A; resistor II = 1.0 A; resistor IV = 500 mA; battery = 1.0 A

36c PD across AB: 6.0 V (use $V = IR$); across BC also 6.0 V (same reason); across CF is 3.0 V (use
$V = IR$); across FG is zero (no resistance between the points), and across AG is 15 V (same as the battery)

37a

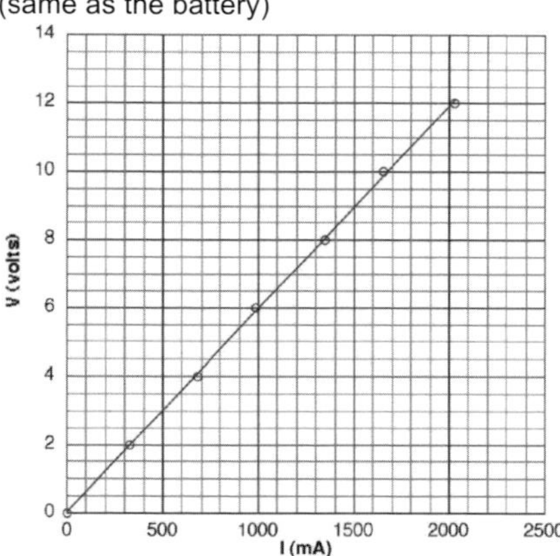

37b 5.6 ohm — Average resistance is the gradient of the graph (can be used here because fuse wire is clearly ohmic).

37c The linear nature of the graph indicates that it is ohmic.

37d 11.2 ohm (resistors in series add their resistance).

37e 2.8 ohm (identical resistors in parallel have half resistance of one resistor, since the current will double for the same voltage).

38

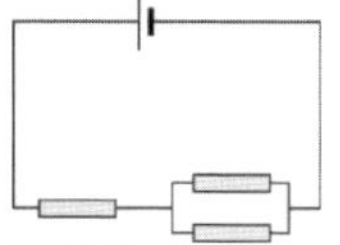

39a	0.20 A	In parallel with and same value as resistor D
39b	0.20 A	In parallel with and same value as resistor D
39c	0.60 A	They are all in series and all the currents through C, D and E must travel through them.
39d	1.0 V	They are all in parallel; use $V = IR$
39e	10 V	Must be the sum of voltages across A, B, F and the combination of C, D and E = 3 + 3+ 3 + 1
40a	3.0 V	Total PD across the two resistors = 6.0 V (note one battery is reversed and 'cancels out' one more).
40b	1.7 Ω	Current through every part of this series circuit is 1.8 A; $V = IR$

41 • In circuit (A), the ammeter will short circuit both resistors and flatten the battery. quickly

• In circuit (B), the voltmeter is correctly connected to read the PD across the two resistors.

• In circuit (C), the voltmeter will block current through the upper resistor, but the ammeter is correctly connected to read the current through the other resistor. The voltmeter will in fact read the battery PD.

• In circuit (D), current will only flow through the lower resistor; the ammeter will correctly measure this current.

42 30 kW h — 1 kW h = 3.6 MJ

43 12.5 A Total power drain is 150 W; now use $P = VI$

44

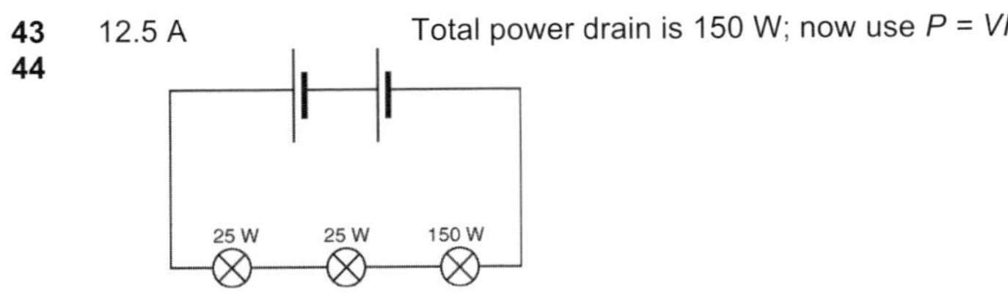

Chapter 13 Magnetism

1 D The magnetic fields from the two magnets cancel at that point.

2 D A parallel magnetic alignment of neighbouring atoms occurs.

3a B The magnetic fields add.

3b A The magnetic fields would now cancel.

4 A The magnetic fields add at the central point, but the AC current in the coils ensures they keep swapping direction from left to right to left to right.

5 B The solenoid on the left will have an S pole near the bar magnet, and the solenoid on the right will have an N pole near the bar magnet. This will push the N pole of the bar magnet towards the left i.e. anti-clockwise.

6 Iron, nickel, cobalt are (ferro-)magnetic metals. Some forms of steel are magnetic, while others are not. Aluminium, copper, lead, tin, titanium, zinc, gold, silver and platinum are not magnetic metals.

7

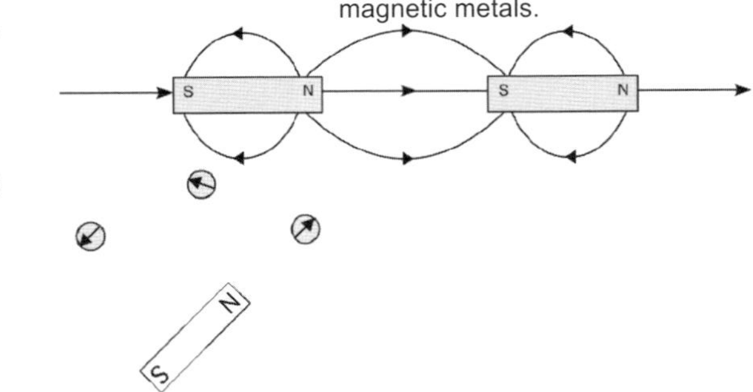

8

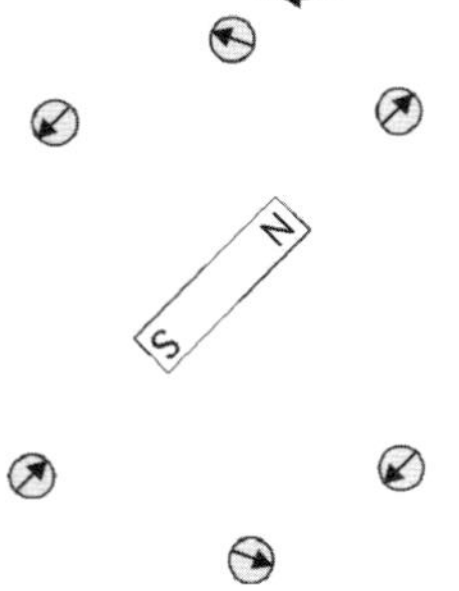

9 It will point NW.

10 The Earth's magnetic pole in the north is of the same kind as a south pole in a bar magnet; and the Earth's magnetic pole in the south is of the same kind as a north pole in a bar magnet.

11 The magnetic field patterns are virtually identical in shape. The solenoid appears to have a south pole at one end and a north pole at the other. The field lines inside the solenoid can be visualised in a way not possible with a bar magnet – though the magnetic field lines inside a bar magnet are of the same shape. Perhaps the major differences are that it is possible to change the strength of the magnetic field of a solenoid by simply changing the current through it, and it is possible to produce an 'AC' magnetic field with a solenoid by using AC electricity.

12

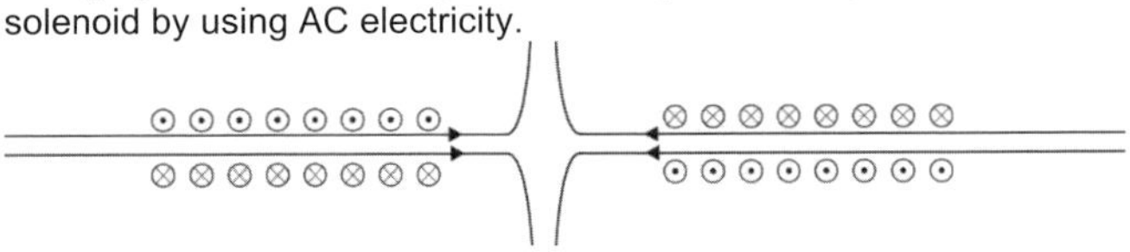

13

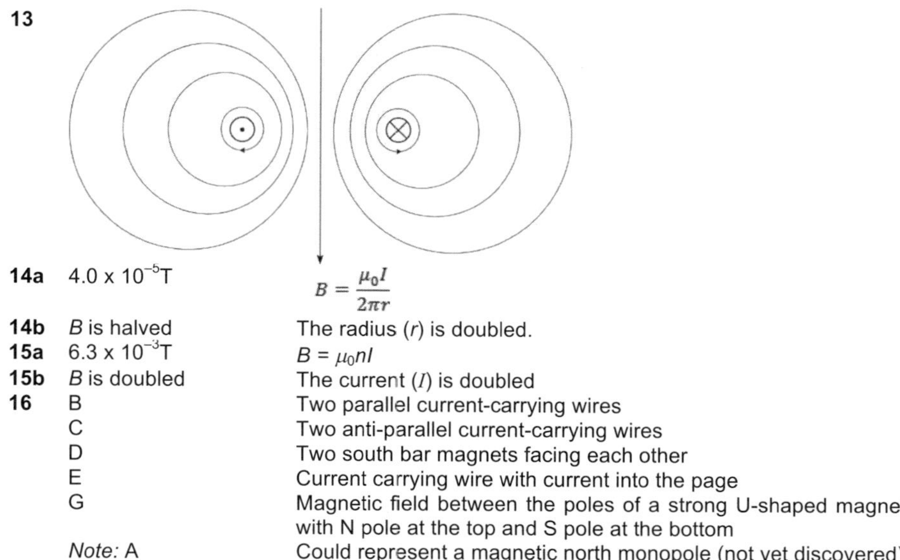

14a 4.0×10^{-5} T — $B = \frac{\mu_0 I}{2\pi r}$

14b *B* is halved — The radius (r) is doubled.

15a 6.3×10^{-3} T — $B = \mu_0 n I$

15b *B* is doubled — The current (I) is doubled

16

B	Two parallel current-carrying wires
C	Two anti-parallel current-carrying wires
D	Two south bar magnets facing each other
E	Current carrying wire with current into the page
G	Magnetic field between the poles of a strong U-shaped magnet with N pole at the top and S pole at the bottom
Note: A	Could represent a magnetic north monopole (not yet discovered)
Note: F	Field lines cannot cross each other.

Data Sheet

Earth's gravitational acceleration, g	$9.8\ \text{m s}^{-2}$
Earth's gravitational field, g	$9.8\ \text{N kg}^{-1}$
Speed of light, c	$3.00 \times 10^{8}\ \text{m s}^{-2}$
Magnetic force constant, $(k = \frac{\mu_0}{2\pi})$	$2.0 \times 10^{-7}\ \text{N A}^{-2}$
Coulomb force constant, $(k = \frac{1}{4\pi\varepsilon_0})$	$9.0 \times 10^{9}\ \text{N m}^{2}\ \text{C}^{-2}$
Density of water, ρ	$1.00 \times 10^{3}\ \text{kg m}^{-3}$
Specific heat capacity of water	$4.18 \times 10^{3}\ \text{J kg}^{-1}\ \text{K}^{-1}$
Latent heat of fusion of water	$3.34 \times 10^{5}\ \text{J K}^{-1}$
Latent heat of vaporisation of water	$2.26 \times 10^{6}\ \text{J K}^{-1}$
Melting point of ice	273 K
Boiling point of water	373 K
Absolute zero	–273 °C
Charge on electron	$-1.602 \times 10^{-19}\ \text{C}$
Charge on proton	$+1.602 \times 10^{-19}\ \text{C}$

Notes

Notes

Notes

Notes

Notes

Notes